UNDERSTANDING
CHRISTIAN
SPIRITUALITY

Michael Downey

PAULIST PRESS
New York / Mahwah, N.J.

Cover design by Jim Brisson.

Library of Congress Cataloging-in-Publication Data

Downey, Michael.
    Understanding Christian spirituality / Michael Downey.
        p.   cm.
    Includes bibliographical references and index.
    ISBN 0-8091-3680-5 (alk. paper)
    1. Spirituality—Catholic   Church.   2. Catholic   Church—Doctrines.
    I. Title.
    BX2350.65.D68 1996
    248—dc20   96-41355
                                                                   CIP

Published by Paulist Press
997 Macarthur Boulevard
Mahwah, New Jersey 07430

Contents

IN MEMORY OF MY BELOVED GRANDMOTHER

Mary Ann Boyce McCauley
18 August 1899 – 9 October 1995

The sufferings we now endure bear no comparison with the
glory, as yet unrevealed, which is in store for us.
Romans 8:18

Introduction

The richness of words rests in their capacity to trigger many meanings. A word's meaning depends on the context in which it is used. The word *love* may mean many things, depending on the frame of reference. Some people say that they love ice cream. Others love the weather in Hawaii. For others still, "love" is a term reserved to describe the deepest affective response of the human person to another.

In the church emerging from the Second Vatican Council, *experience* and *community* have become key terms in the Christian vocabulary. And though they are used with great frequency in church circles, their meanings are often very hazy. *Spirituality* is another such word. Like *love, experience,* and *community,* it conveys a sometimes staggering multiplicity of meanings. The purpose of this book is to bring some light on the question: What is spirituality? And: What is Christian spirituality?

The interest in spirituality today is on the rise and extends well beyond the parameters of Christianity. My perspective on this new wave of interest in spirituality is colored by the fact that I am a Christian and a Roman Catholic theologian. And so my point of view is necessarily limited. The understanding of spirituality developed in these pages is shaped by Christian convictions. My concern is to engage in a discussion about the nature and scope of a specifically Christian spirituality. But I strive to do this in view of the larger currents and movements in spirituality in the present, both religious and nonreligious.

I anticipate that this book will be of interest primarily to Christians, particularly Roman Catholics, who are trying to understand what people mean when they are speaking about spirituality today. It is written with upper-level college students and entry-level graduate students in mind, as well as for parish study groups, people doing retreat work and spiritual direction, and those involved in the various steps and stages of Christian initiation. But it is also intended for all those who want to understand the distinctive elements of a Christian spirituality in light of the larger scene in contemporary spirituality.

Chapter 1 provides a survey of spirituality in our day, and offers an explanation of some of the reasons why there is such an eruption of interest in the spiritual. It is in this chapter that I offer an explanation of what is meant by the term "spirituality" in the hope of clarifying its nature and scope without tying down its meaning.

The second chapter addresses the issue of a specifically Christian spirituality in light of the universal quest for personal integration through knowledge, freedom, and love. With an eye to the great diversity of spiritualities to which life in Christ gives rise, I explain some of the language central to Christian spirituality: Spirit; Holy Spirit; Spirit of God, Spirit of Christ.

In the third chapter I stipulate that any authentic Christian spirituality is expressed in relationship to tradition. Drawing attention to the all-too-common tendency today to view the Christian tradition in a naive and romanticized manner, I suggest a more sober reading of this tradition and a critical relationship to it so as to fashion a Christian response appropriate to the urgent demands of our age, as well as to fashion a viable future within this living tradition.

Chapter 4 treats some of the central affirmations of the Second Vatican Council as the orienting principles of a renewed Christian spirituality: The centrality of the Word in scripture; the foundational and formative role of liturgy; the universal call to holiness; the Spirit's presence in both church and world.

Chapter 5 provides a survey of the most noteworthy currents in Christian spirituality today as an indication of the shape which spirituality is taking on the brink of the third millennium. Not all currents in Christian spirituality are expressive of authentic development, and so it is necessary here to address some of the problems which continue to dog those who strive to live in Christ in today's church and world.

One of the most important developments in Christian spirituality is the emergence of a distinct discipline for the study of this subject. In chapter 6 I offer an explanation of the four major methods for the study of Christian spirituality, and attend to five other approaches which are still growing to full stature in the effort to understand Christian spirituality.

The final chapter spells out the salient features of a contemporary Christian spirituality, and offers guiding principles to assist those seeking to understand and live a Christian spirituality informed by tradition as well as by the continuing presence and action of the Spirit in human life, history, world, and church.

It is a delight to acknowledge my indebtedness to those who have been helpful to me in the course of my research and writing. The first word of gratitude is extended to the Cistercian monks of Mepkin Abbey in South Carolina, whose home became mine while I was writing. Through the gracious and generous hospitality of Francis Kline, Abbot of Mepkin, I was able to share fully in the monastic rhythm of prayer and work. At Mepkin I had occasion to discuss the work-in-progress with the monks in formation. Their careful observations and constructive criticism helped me to clarify some of my thinking on the subject at hand. Fred Heckel and Dale Bennett read the entire manuscript and offered an encouraging word.

Next, I must express my thanks to Bellarmine College for awarding me a research grant which provided the opportunity to concentrate on this work.

Several colleagues in the field of spirituality agreed to offer a careful reading of the work, and I thank them: Regina Bechtle, Kathleen Deignan, Bruce Lescher, and James Wiseman. Thomas Rausch, colleague and friend over the years and across the miles, has been consistently supportive of my approach to the study of spirituality.

Mark O'Keefe took to heart the words of St. Benedict: "Let all guests be received as Christ." His kind hospitality made it possible for me to bring this work to completion without interruption or further delay.

Richard Sparks, editor at Paulist Press, has exercised a lion's share of patience in the face of the many unexpected delays along the way.

Kathleen Walsh at Paulist Press saw the project through its last stages.

To one and all, my deep and abiding gratitude.

CHAPTER 1

Spirituality Today

It is quite common to hear that people today experience a deep spiritual hunger. But those familiar with spiritual traditions whose roots are long, deep, and strong know that this is nothing new. What is intriguing from any point of view, however, is the great variety of ways in which people are satisfying this hunger. The best-seller lists of the 1990s provide a sampling of the fare. Titles like *Women Who Run With the Wolves* by Clarissa Pinkola Estes, James Redfield's *The Celestine Prophecy* and Betty J. Eadie's *Embraced by the Light* have shown surprising staying power. Then there is Marianne Williamson's *Return to Love*, and her *Illuminata: Thoughts, Prayers, Rites of Passage*. Williamson has found her niche in the new spirituality Hall of Fame alongside other notables such as M. Scott Peck. Arguably the most important entry in the spirituality "Hall of Fame" during the 1990s, however, is Thomas Moore, whose phenomenally successful *Care of the Soul* is thought by some to be a spiritual masterpiece. This is to say nothing of the bumper crop of books on angels which cram the shelves of local booksellers. Though not a book on spirituality properly speaking, it is worth noting that John Paul II's *Crossing the Threshold of Hope* knocked the new spirituality writers down a rung or two as it climbed to the top of the charts in the mid-1990s.

Browsers and buyers at Waldenbooks, Crown Books, B. Dalton, Barnes & Noble or another large bookseller downtown or at the nearest shopping mall will have noticed significant changes in the bookshops' offerings. If your interest is in "spirituality," the first stop will likely be that nook labelled "inspiration." No doubt there will be a few Bibles from which to choose, a sampling of Judaica, and perhaps some M. Scott Peck and Thomas Moore. There will probably be a smattering of the growing literature on near-death experiences, and a few titles dealing with different approaches to meditation rooted in the religions of the East. These days it's likely that there will be several copies of Joseph F. Girzone's *Joshua* and some of his lesser known works. You may find various titles based on *A Course in Miracles*. From time to time there will be a few books by or about Gethsemani's most celebrated son, Thomas Merton. If there is time and you still have the stamina, a closer look may yield yet more of this spiritual fare on some of the other shelves. Try "history," "self-help," "women's studies," "biography," "relationships," or some of the other categories. It's everywhere.

The focus of many new books in "spirituality" or "inspiration" is, to put it simply, the soul and the sacred. Much of the new spirituality is concerned with addressing the loss of soul so pervasive in contemporary Western cultures. Different spiritual writers offer various solutions for filling the void. In many instances, the resolution has to do with a recovery of an awareness of the sacred, but the meanings of the term "sacred" are quite vague. Whether any one of these representatives of the new quest is on sure footing is arguable. What seems beyond dispute, however, is that great numbers of people today recognize that we have a glut of material things, too much "stuff," but are still deeply unsatisfied. There is an ache in the soul, a longing for more than meets the eye.

Publishers who are in any way involved with the "religion product" boast that some of their best-selling titles are those dealing with spirituality and inspiration. Gallup studies have projected that the largest sales increase in nonfiction books in the twenty-first century will be in religion/spirituality. The projection is that there will be an 82 percent growth in these books between 1987 and 2010.

SPIRITUAL TRENDS TODAY

The interest in spirituality manifests itself in ways beyond counting. Most of these give cause for delight and for hope. Others give reason for caution, while others still are alarming.

This is due to the fact that "spirituality" is used in speaking about practices of prayer and devotion as well as practices associated with the occult. "Spirituality" may describe the fascination with appearances of the Virgin Mary and at the same time refer to extraordinary phenomena such as the preservation of the buried bodies of saints from corruption. "Spirituality" is sometimes used to describe a people's practices of voodoo or witchcraft, as well as their preoccupation with evil spirits. "Spirituality" may be the word to describe a commitment to naturopathic medicine or other practices of healing and wholeness. For some, a rigorous regime of exercise, meditation, and organic diet is a spiritual discipline.

In these days of cable television, there is a glut of purveyors of products intended to improve self-image, often packaged in the language of "feel-good" spirituality. In recent years there has been the emergence of the secular retreat movement promoted by businesses and corporate executives for the purpose of strengthening personal growth in and through corporate identity and increased productivity. In most of these developments there is a sharp line drawn between spirituality and religion. Together with this is an implicit or explicit conviction that spirituality is what really matters. Religion and adherence to the beliefs of a religious tradition may be helpful, but are certainly not essential in cultivating a spiritual life. In the process, religion, religious traditions, and religious affiliation are subtly denigrated. Such tendencies are often at the heart of some of the more significant movements in spirituality in North America.

Certainly, one of the most notable trends today is the spirituality referred to as New Age. New Age spirituality seems to apply to just about anything new. But it also refers to the not-so-new. It covers gazing at crystal balls, pop psychologies, interest in organic gardening, eating organically-grown foods, holistic health programs, clairvoyance, and the development of self-help skills. New Age bears positive connotations for its advocates, and negative ones for its opponents. For some, centering prayer is New Age, as is any talk of divinization of the human person, even though the notion of gradual divinization by grace has firm roots in early Christian traditions. For still others New Age covers anything from practices of transcendental meditation, Zen prayer disciplines, T'ai Chi, Ira Progoff's intensive journaling methods, acupuncture, naturopathic medicine, reliance on guided imagery in prayer, dreamwork, Jungian psychology of any sort, Enneagram-related prayer and spirituality, and anything even remotely associated with Matthew Fox and creation-centered spirituality. New Age spirituality appears to have room for gazing at stars and different sorts of rocks and colored stones which are thought to provide access to spiritual realities. Then there is channelling, Wicca cults, and fascination with Satan and the demonic. Even contemporary California "muzak" released under the Windham Hill label, as well as other sorts of soft music, is often described as New Age.

Some see in these trends a corruption of authentic spirituality. Many view New Age as a dabbling in the eclectic and esoteric. Not a few individuals and religious groups judge it to be a flagrant manifestation of the antichrist. But New Age is rather more a spiritual smorgasbord, a sort of salad bar approach to spirituality which invites a nibble here and there on whatever suits one's taste. Yet what is called for in the face of it all is a good measure of discrimination and restraint.

A second overarching current in contemporary spirituality is the increased appreciation of the importance of psychological insights in the spiritual quest. Since spirituality is not concerned in the first place with religious beliefs or obligations but with the *experience* of the sacred precisely *as experience*, psychological investigations are judged to be very helpful in the task of spiritual development. This awareness is rooted in the recognition that human and spiritual development are not opposing, competing dynamics, but are interrelated and complementary. At the risk of oversimplification, there is a fairly reliable rule of thumb: Human growth and maturation are prerequisites for growing and maturing in the spiritual life. This is not a hard and fast rule. But immaturity, irresponsibility, brute exercises of power, and irrational behavior should signal caution, even and especially when appeal is made to a higher order or spiritual principle in an effort to justify them.

Such an appreciation of psychological investigations in relation to the spiritual quest has resulted in what some see as the "psychologization" of spirituality. It often appears that the therapeutic is the governing category in spirituality today. Indeed it must be noted that such currents influenced by psychology run the risk of giving rise to self-absorption, self-preoccupation, self-fixation, even where the focus on the self is aimed at improving relationships with others. The criticism that much contemporary spirituality is mute on issues of social justice, political responsibility, and economic accountability is not without warrant.

A third noteworthy trend in spirituality today is the turn to the East for inspiration and practical guidance. There is widespread fascination with what is often perceived to be the simple wisdom of the East. The spiritual traditions of the East, especially Zen practices, are particularly attractive because of what are often naively thought to be simple methods of meditation, disciplines of mind and body, and insights about the role of the body and various body postures in bringing clarity and focus to one's day-to-day living. Many find in the wisdom of the East a source of strength for convictions which are already held, whereas for others this wisdom brings fresh insight and an altogether different view of the world and of the sacred. For many Christians, Thomas Merton serves as an exemplar of a Christian whose own commitments were enhanced by the rich spiritual traditions he encountered in his turn to the East.

There is as well a strong interest in the spirituality of Native American peoples. Indeed there are noble traditions here. But far too often these peoples and their heritage are viewed in a romanticized and naive fashion by contemporary people on the spiritual quest, what might be referred to as the "Dances With Wolves Syndrome." The spiritual legacies of these peoples are interpreted selectively, and popularized to suit contemporary tastes, particularly the preferences of North Americans disaffected by institutional religion. Though much of the interest in and enthusiasm for these venerable spiritualities is often naive and romanticized, this should not obscure the fact that there is an abundance of serious and sober appreciation for them and other spiritual traditions less commonly known to people in the contemporary West.

A fourth development is related to the third. Perhaps one of the greatest riches of the spiritual traditions of the East and of the Native Americans is their deep appreciation for the sacredness of the earth. Contemporary Westerners, particularly North Americans, are being enriched by the wisdom of Native American peoples which recognizes the presence of the sacred in the earth, in nonhuman life, and in the elements. As we approach the turn of the century, there is ever-increasing attention to the urgent necessity to protect, preserve, and care for the earth and its life systems. The threat of nuclear annihilation, and the destruction of the ecological balance through systematic ravaging of the earth's resources, has caused some to be particularly mindful of the value and dignity of other forms of life, and to work for the creation of a just and nonviolent way of living with other species and those life forms upon which humans depend for their very existence. This is a hopeful development in contemporary spirituality, one which can serve as a corrective to those approaches to spirituality which tend to be so focused on personal growth and development to the neglect of our relationship to all other creatures.

The fifth and perhaps most noteworthy current in spirituality in the United States today is the proliferation of various self-help movements. Consider the various movements inspired by the Twelve Steps of Alcoholics Anonymous. Many have found inspiration and practical guidance in the Twelve Steps, struggling to live one day at a time through the process of lifelong surrender to a Higher Power. Some suggest that the spirituality of the Twelve Steps will be the most enduring legacy of the twentieth century United States to the great spiritual traditions.

Indeed there has been a veritable explosion of Twelve Step, codependency, and recovery-related programs whose primary purpose is "self-help." "How-to," "healing," and "self-help" programs of all sorts are flourishing everywhere to assist people with grief, loss, divorce, the trauma of sexual abuse, coping with stress, and so forth. The primary aim of these programs is healing or wellness through gradual recovery from the effects of an illness, addiction, compulsion, or some other negative factor which has caused one's life to become unmanageable. Though many in these programs often express interest in and commitment to spirituality in contrast to religion, others within and outside the programs question whether the Twelve Steps and related movements are really spiritual at all. One might ask whether the language of addiction, dependency and codependency has been used so loosely as to lack any coherent meaning. For example, is it really appropriate to speak of being addicted to television, or to work, or to print? When someone says "I'm addicted to print," she means to say that she loves to read. And this is very different from, say, being addicted to crack cocaine.

Perhaps it is because the Twelve Steps of AA have been such a source of healing, wellness, and integration for so many that others who suffer from the effects of innumerable negative factors in their lives see in the wisdom of the Twelve Steps a rich resource for spiritual growth and transformation. But those within Alcoholics Anonymous itself often express reservations about the application of their steps, principles, and traditions so broadly to persons facing any and all kinds of problems. When the Twelve-Step language is used so broadly and loosely as to apply to countless numbers of persons, groups, and institutions, does it then lose its capacity to express an authentic spirituality? Or is there a formula regarding dysfunction that is useful in any system?[1]

A final current that deserves greater attention than we are able to provide here is the emergence of feminist spirituality and likewise masculine spirituality. Feminist spirituality will be described more fully later in this work, but it is important to note at the outset its significance along with the men's movement and masculine spirituality as major trends in the development of spirituality today.

Phyllis A. Tickle, religion editor of the publishing and book-selling trade journal *Publishers Weekly*, has provided an instructive survey of the recent trends in the publishing and selling of books by both secular and religious publishers.[2] By attending to recent patterns in the book industry, Tickle draws some helpful conclusions about spirituality, religion, and the sacred in the United States today. Her judgment is that we in the U.S. are undergoing a second Reformation in our understanding and practice of religion and spirituality. Her insights may be instructive about spiritual trends in the United States and beyond.

Tickle groups the growing literature on spirituality into four general categories. This categorization helps identify several convictions about spirituality held by the American people on the basis of the kinds of books they are buying and reading.

First, people believe in the sacred, and that it is possible for them to encounter it. What they mean by "sacred" is often quite unclear. But, in addition to belief in the sacred there is the belief that the sacred is searching us out. This is evident in the growing literature about near-death experiences, angels, miracles, and prophecies.

Second, people today are seeking well-worn ways of wisdom. There is a longing for spiritualities that have stood the test of time. At the root of this there is a desire for what was once known but now seems to have been lost. This may be seen in the efforts to recover the historical Jesus,[3] to provide a bare bones portrait of the man Jesus prior to the emergence of the Christian tradition which, many feel, clouds rather than clarifies his meaning and message. It is also seen in the turn to the age-old spiritual wisdom of the East, and to the reserves of Native American wisdom from ages prior to European colonization. Further, many are drawn to such books as the *Catechism of the Catholic Church* which is viewed as a sort of compendium of the tried and true wisdom of the Catholic tradition.

Third, there is the belief that people must take personal responsibility for their own lives. This is apparent in the wave of interest in the self-help movement inspired by the Twelve Steps of Alcoholics Anonymous. At the heart of this movement and the various programs inspired by it is the conviction that people have gotten themselves into whatever ails them, and that their ills can only be remedied once they make a personal decision to adopt right beliefs and right attitudes as the basis for right behavior.

Fourth, people today are drawn to stories, simple stories which embody straightforward, uncomplicated messages. Simple, practical stories like Joseph Girzone's *Joshua*, or Robert Fulghum's *All I Really Needed to Know I Learned in Kindergarten*, or those in William J. Bennett's *The Book of Virtues: A Treasury of the World's Great Moral Stories* have enormous appeal to great numbers of readers, no doubt as an antidote to the stress and tension many feel as a result of living in a highly complex and demanding world.

Tickle's typology is instructive in many ways. But more telling for our purposes is her use of the terms "sacred," "spirituality," and "religion." For Tickle, the sacred is common to all men and women, and accessible to all. It is "a structured given in our being."[4] Like our cardiovascular system or the sun, the sacred is a "given" in life and, like them, is perceived but not embraced. Spirituality is more subjective than religion. It is "an attitude about the sacred and a set of personal choices and disciplines for living in accord with it."[5] If spirituality is subjective, religion is objective, external, less personal, "as much a man-made construct as a god-made one."[6] It is a means of interpreting history, both personal and communal, and of ordering our choices.

Tickle's definitions of the sacred, spirituality, and religion are all quite hazy. But in this she is representative of many Americans for whom "spirituality," "sacred," and "religion" are all very fuzzy. Their meanings are vague, vexing, and vast. Though there may be disagreement over the precise meaning of "spirituality," it is beyond dispute that we are witnessing a tidal wave of interest in it. People of all sorts, even those who are not religious in the ordinary understanding of the term, seem to be grappling with the deepest yearnings in the human heart, a desire for more than meets the eye—for the sacred. One way of "naming" this desire for the more, for the greater, for things unseen—for the sacred, is to speak of spirituality, the spiritual, the spiritual life.

WHAT *IS* SPIRITUALITY?

At this point, we must face a singularly important question and face it head-on. It is a question which is unresolved in so much of the contemporary discussion about spirituality. The question is this: Just what *is* spirituality?

In much the same way that the bookseller or the librarian must make judgments about exactly where to shelve books for those interested in spirituality, we must make some hard judgments about what we mean when we use the term. For all the interest in spirituality today, there remains a lack of precision about what people mean when they speak of spirituality.

In view of this tidal wave, this spiritual sprawl, what is needed is a clear definition of spirituality, one which would allow enough room for all that is authentic in the quest for the sacred, while at the same time providing some criteria for discernment in the face of the many instances of human self-expression now huddling under that umbrella-like term "spirituality."

In moving toward a clear definition, it may be helpful to note that in the various spiritual movements today there appear to be two strands which run throughout. First, and most importantly, there is an awareness that there are levels of reality not immediately apparent; there is more than meets the eye. Second, there is a quest for personal integration in the face of forces of fragmentation and depersonalization. In my view, these are the two spirituality constants, the two essential components in any approach to spirituality.

The term "spirituality" is used by some to describe the depth dimension of all human existence. Here the emphasis is on spirituality as a constitutive element of human nature and experience. Joann Wolski Conn speaks of spirituality in terms of the capacity for self-transcendence.[7] For Ewert Cousins, spirituality refers to "the inner dimension of the person...[where] ultimate reality is experienced."[8] John Macquarrie understands spirituality to be concerned with "becoming a person in the fullest sense."[9] For Gordon Wakefield, spirituality has to do with "the constituent of human nature which seeks relations with the ground or purpose of existence."[10] Edward Kinerk envisions spirituality as the expression of the dialectic by which one moves from the inauthentic to the authentic.[11] Perhaps the most open-ended formulation of all comes from Raimundo Panikkar who speaks of spirituality as "one typical way of handling the human condition."[12]

When viewed in this broad sense of the term, "spirituality" is used to describe an element in human experience precisely as experience and precisely as human. Spirituality here refers to the authentic human quest for ultimate value, or the human person's "striving to attain the highest ideal or goal."[13] Spirituality of whatever kind in this very broad sense of the term concerns a "progressive, consciously pursued, personal integration through self-transcendence within and toward the horizon of ultimate concern."[14]

Some of those referred to above are engaged in the rigorous study of spirituality. Sandra Schneiders, one of the most significant voices in this line of study, has argued persuasively in favor of a broadly-based approach to spirituality. In this perspective, there are many different kinds of spirituality, some of which may have no explicit reference to God. These may be authentic spiritualities nonetheless, "spiritual" here referring to the realization or actualization of the human spirit. For Schneiders, spirituality in the broadest sense refers to "the experience of consciously striving to integrate one's life in terms not of isolation and self-absorption but of self-transcendence toward the ultimate value one perceives."[15] As an example of a nonreligious spirituality, consider a person who devotes his or her life to the pursuit of peace and justice, bringing all of a life's energies to bear on the pursuit of these values. In Schneiders' view, such a person might be living a spirituality of peace and justice, even though there may be in his or her life no recognition of the existence of God. Similarly one may give one's life to the promotion of a feminist agenda, working toward the full equality of women and men in every sphere of life. Schneiders' position would allow for the possibility of such a feminist spirituality, whether God is in the picture or not.

Schneiders' rigorous investigations lead us to conclude that spirituality is a way of consciously striving to integrate one's life through self-transcending knowledge, freedom and love in light of the highest values perceived and pursued. But the personal integration at issue here, one of the two spirituality constants I have identified, is all the more pressing because of the degree of depersonalization and fragmentation which so many of us experience today.

WHY SPIRITUALITY *TODAY?*

Why is there such an enormous degree of interest in spirituality today? What are the reasons for this renaissance of interest in spirituality? There are several momentous events in the history of our own century that have brought about a sea change in our understanding. There is, of course, the Holocaust of the Jews and six million others. Then there is the horror of Hiroshima, the first instance of massive nuclear destruction. These profoundly interruptive and disorienting events, and others that continue to riddle our lives and histories as persons and as a people, have altered our conception of the sacred. For example, prior to

August 6, 1945, cataclysmic destruction was understood to be the prerogative of divine power. But with Hiroshima, destruction took the form of annihilation at the hands of human beings. For many, Hiroshima put a bold question mark before God. Because if God is not in charge, controlling everything in existence, then everything may be random and absurd. With Hiroshima comes a rupture between God and what really matters. For many people today, what matters is this life and it alone. As a result, our ways of understanding the sacred have begun to change. Americans have yet to reckon with the political, moral, cultural, humanitarian, and religious consequences of that first massive nuclear destruction. The same is true for Auschwitz.[16]

As I see it, Auschwitz and Hiroshima together are the most formative religious events of the twentieth century. Ironically they are demonic, not divine. In the aftermath of these two instances of horror, the cloud and the pillar of fire no longer evoke the redemptive grace of the Exodus. Instead they remind us of the curls of smoke from the crematoria at Auschwitz and the white mushroom clouds of Hiroshima and Nagasaki. Auschwitz and Hiroshima manifest the demonic result of the sacralization of violence and war. In the decisions and actions which led up to these horrific events, the human will was gradually surrendered in unquestioning obedience to a higher authority of near-sacral proportions. The surrender to authority in religious obedience of this sort then absolves the agent of responsibility for one's action. In the aftermath of these two horrors, there is among many a strong conviction that there can be no unwavering obedience to any sacred authority, even God.

It is our profound awareness of evil in the twentieth century that has the most profound implications for spirituality today. This must be understood in light of our scientific and technological hubris which has had the disastrous consequences of Auschwitz, Hiroshima and more. It is *human* agency adrift from God which is *the* critical issue as well as God's apparent silence and powerlessness in the face of human arrogance and evil.

In addition to the horror of the Holocaust, Hiroshima, and the whole host of historical events so profoundly interruptive and disjunctive, particular attention must be drawn to the American involvement in Vietnam which has resulted in shifting understandings of spirituality, the sacred and, especially, religion. Many Americans learned an important lesson from U.S. involvement in Vietnam: There is reason to be suspicious of authority. As a consequence, for many, authority of all kinds is subject to critique, even and especially religious authority, precisely because of the measure of obedience it requires. This distrust and distaste for authority, brought on in a singular way by American involvement in Vietnam, was deepened by the assassinations in the U.S. and abroad in the 1960s, by the egregious abuses of power and authority uncovered in the Civil Rights movement, and by the betrayal of authority and power signalled in the Watergate scandal. And there is more. The list seems endless. All authoritative statements, directives, explanations, and defenses are under suspicion.

One of the results of the shock of history, of what actually goes on in the world, is a turn inward, a greater reliance on the self because of the unreliability of outer worlds of meaning and purpose and value which external authorities are intended to uphold and safeguard. The final arbiter of right and wrong, good and evil, comes to be one's own feelings about things. One's own perception, standing on one's own two feet, becomes the sole gauge for commitment, moral responsibility, and sound judgment. And, perhaps most important, it becomes the litmus test for one's belief in the sacred. It is then a very short step toward the conviction, now deeply and widely held, that belief in God and adherence to religious principles is purely a matter of personal taste and pleasure, or of personal experience.

The Holocaust, Hiroshima, and Vietnam are three of the most important factors which have caused the shift in our understanding of spirituality, religion, and the sacred. More positively, much could be said about the impact of the space age and the advance of telecommunications on our understanding. Taken as a whole, however, the momentous events of the twentieth century have caused people to feel that they have been cut loose from those past securities which provided them with a sense of meaning, purpose, and value. We have been wrenched from our moorings by the horrors and terrors of the twentieth century. The Einsteinian relativity revolution has dislocated us from our setting in a more manageable universe. The sheer quantum leap in science and technology has altered our ways of being in the world and relating to it and to each other. Add to these historical events the personal tragedies we all face—the untimely death of a loved one, the onset of illness, the randomness of senseless violence, or debilitation due to accident. The cumulative effect is that people today are far more ambivalent about what were once tightly held religious beliefs and convictions about God. They are seeking new ways of recognizing, "naming," and living with an awareness of the sacred.

In addition to these profoundly interruptive and disorienting historical events, there are other influences in our culture which, in my view, may be even more the cause of the current spirituality sprawl. The diagnosis of the current cultural climate in the West provided by Ronald Rolheiser is most instructive in understanding why so many people today are exploring spirituality.[17]

Rolheiser, a Canadian, contends that there are forces in the contemporary culture which have wounded us deeply. These forces are of recent vintage, especially prevalent in Western culture since the Enlightenment. In brief, these forces have afflicted us with three major problems: narcissism, pragmatism, and unbridled restlessness.

As a result of these influences, many of us in the cultures of the West are inclined to think of ourselves first and foremost as individuals with the ability to reason. The understanding of reason here is restricted and restricting insofar as it is understood preeminently in terms of the human capacity for logical analysis. Following the Enlightenment, our concern has been with individual rights and liberties, and with the capacity to give shape to ourselves and our destinies. We think of persons, ourselves and others, as individuated centers of consciousness. We strive for self-sufficiency and self-determination as if these were the principal purposes of personal development. In this view, we are individuals before we are community. We are selves prior to being in communion with others. In Rolheiser's telling, this is a thoroughly modern understanding of the human person. And it lends itself all too easily to self-preoccupation, self-absorption, self-fixation. Briefly, our culture cultivates individualism and breeds narcissism.

North Americans are, if nothing else, pragmatists. This has its advantages, to be sure. We work hard. We tend to be efficient. We get things done. But the flip side of this is that we tend to be overly concerned with results, with outcomes we can measure and assess. So many of us are impatient with theories and ideas. We deplore ivory tower speculation. In the North American frame of mind, the truth is what works. And if it works it must be true. We say "the proof is in the pudding." We judge persons by what they do. We value people because of their achievements. But this tendency poses a real difficulty in our quest for the sacred, because the sacred will not succumb to our instruments of assessment. In living the spiritual life there is no "bottom line." The spiritual life, authentically lived, is a most impractical thing to do. Imagine, monks rising at three in the morning to sing psalms! What's the use?

In addition to breeding narcissism and bottom-line pragmatism, the culture in which we live instills in us an unbridled restlessness. We are hungry for experience. We want to go places, see things, do things. The refrain heard frequently enough these days says it all: "Been there, done that." So we move on to the next thing. But speed kills!

Our lives are filled with cacophony and clutter. In most of our homes, the television is our constant companion. We are afraid to be alone. We cannot keep still. Put briefly, we need constant excitement and diversion. Even while walking in the park or by the lake or the sea, we fill our ears with the music or the news or the trashy talk show via Walkman.

Today there is a dawning realization that the culture spawned in the Enlightenment has sold us a bill of goods. We've been had. The culture that breeds narcissism, pragmatism, and unbridled restlessness is a dead end, and this is being learned at great personal cost to individuals, communities, and nations. It is my view that people today are beginning to realize that this kind of culture does not work. It has betrayed us. It has not delivered on its promise. It has failed to satisfy the deepest desires of the human heart, and it has resulted in fragmentation and depersonalization of a magnitude previously unimagined. We are looking for another way. And this calls for the cultivation of an awareness of levels of reality beyond the self and what is immediately apparent, beyond what is practical, and what keeps us constantly stimulated. The culture in which we live has numbed us to the deep reserves of spirituality within. Fragmentation, alienation, and depersonalization are so all-pervasive and unsatisfying that other ways of perceiving and being in the world have become necessary for our survival. People today are seeking to find those deep reserves of spirituality within because they know that they are trapped by self-centeredness, utilitarianism, and agitation, and have decided that this is simply no way to live.

Narcissism, pragmatism, and restlessness do not wear well in the spiritual life. To live a deeply spiritual life one must cultivate an abiding awareness of levels of reality beyond the self which are not immediately apparent. The self is decentered. There is more than meets the eye. The person of deep spirituality must cease running and be still, restful, receptive to what is. And perhaps most importantly, the person on the spiritual path must be willing to relinquish preoccupation with results. One does not embark on the spiritual way primarily for the purpose of producing certain results or achieving precise outcomes. We cannot easily assess the outcomes, the results, of the spiritual quest. Indeed, there is no "bottom line" in the spiritual life. This is one of the most painful realizations on any authentic spiritual path. It is, in fact, why so few persevere in the spiritual life, and then move on to something else.

ISSUES ARISING FROM OUR CULTURAL CLIMATE

Historical and cultural factors have contributed to the emergence of two significant problems to be faced in spirituality today. First, the depersonalized and fragmented culture in which we live prompts us to seek personal integration in light of levels of reality not immediately apparent, yet we bear the afflictions of the culture even in our approach to spirituality. So much of the literature on spirituality today is focused on the individual, the self, to the neglect of the importance of community and the wider regions of the social order. Indeed, in some circles spirituality has become virtually synonymous with self-help, self-fix. The spiritual journey can become nothing more than a narcissistic ego trip wrapped in the rhetoric of the sacred.

Similarly, in many approaches to spirituality today there is a kind of shopping around from one brand of spiritual experience to another, from workshops on self-improvement, to varieties of herbal medicines and organic diets, to blends of Celtic and Native American spiritualities, to stargazing and colored stones, to the cults of Wicca and the practices of witchery. This may be nothing more than a manifestation of our unbridled restlessness, an unwillingness to settle in to the rigor and tedium of a well-worn spiritual discipline essential to cultivating an awareness of the sacred.

More problematic still is the tendency in many approaches to spirituality today to seek results, to look for changes in our personality or in our ability to relate to others. Many adopt spiritual disciplines and practices because it helps their day go better. If this doesn't work, then it's dropped and another one taken up. The pragmatic mentality is deeply ingrained. We think that growth and development in the spiritual life should make a difference in our lives. We should be better, more effective, and more satisfied. On the contrary, the only reason for embarking on the way of spirituality is for the sake of the sacred itself. In more religious terms, the reason for living the spiritual life is not because it will make me a different or healthier or better person, but simply because God is God.

There is a bind here. The very problems which have led us to seek a new way of perceiving and being in the world are haunting us on the way. And they often prevent us from entering fully and completely into the depths of the spiritual life. A task that awaits us in our common search is to find or make ways of purging ourselves gradually and painfully of the uniquely modern combination of narcissism, restlessness and, above all, bottom line pragmatism which carry over into our search for the sacred, and which shapes much of the terrain of spirituality today. Until we recognize these three elements as the major problem in spirituality today we will be at war with ourselves in our quest to live a deeply spiritual life.[18]

There is yet a second major problem in the mix of spirituality today. This is the sharp separation which is all too often drawn between spirituality and religion. At the core of the American mindset is a sharp contrast between religion and spirituality, together with an implicit judgment that spirituality and the sacred are essential, while religion, perhaps helpful to some, is not necessary to living a deeply spiritual life. In this view religion is incidental, and indeed may be an obstacle in walking a spiritual path. Spirituality is often understood as a very individual, personal, indeed private matter, whereas religion entails participation in the life of a community, in its worship, adhering to its norms and values.

This distinction between religion and spirituality is clearly articulated in the celebrated work of Wade Clark Roof, *A Generation of Seekers*.[19] Religion is often given short shrift. In some currents in spirituality it is baldly denigrated.

The root of the problem lies in a rather narrow understanding of religion. In common sense understanding, "religion" is roughly synonymous with "religious institution." But the institutional dimension is only one element of religion. Many on the spiritual quest today, those who are striving to live a deeply spiritual life, have left religion or the religious institution. In the eyes of a great number of people, the institution has failed to provide them with the kind of supports and resources necessary for authentic spiritual transformation. And so for many, the exodus from religion as institution has been necessary for their spiritual survival.

One purpose of a religious institution is to mediate, or communicate, the experience of the sacred. Such mediation occurs, in part, through the religious body's sacred texts, communal worship, traditions, social arrangements of leadership, authority, governance. The religious institution is at the service of these dimensions which are necessary in the human quest for God, precisely because humans are social, communal beings. When people leave religious institutions because they have been failed or betrayed by them, there is far too often a tendency to think that one can "go it alone" in the spiritual quest. But there remains a need for texts, traditions, structures of community and authority which the religious institution safeguards and serves, albeit sometimes quite poorly. But those who opt out of any religious affiliation are called upon to find other networks of community, tradition, holy writings and so forth, lest the spiritual quest become an individualistic, purely private matter.

Recall that spirituality is concerned with the full range of human experience, every inch and ounce of it, and with integrating the whole of one's life in light of more than meets the eye. And so the need for what religious institutions provide cannot be neglected. Indeed the very premise that the religious and the spiritual are two separate paths, two different options, warrants scrutiny.

Therefore, if it is correct that there are two spirituality constants—(1) the awareness that there are levels of reality not immediately apparent and (2) the search for personal integration because of fragmentation and depersonalization—then adherence to religious beliefs, belonging to a religious tradition, and affiliating with a religious community should not and cannot be ruled out in the quest for integration.

RELIGION AND SPIRITUALITY: TWO PATHS?

A broader view in which religion is not equated with the religious institution has been articulated by the 19th century lay theologian Friedrich von Hügel in *The Mystical Element of Religion*.[20] Put briefly: Humans are intrinsically religious. The religious dimension in us is that which inclines to the sacred and binds us to it. Religion has various elements. Said another way, the religious dimension in us is expressed in different ways. First, there is the institutional dimension wherein our quest for the sacred is formalized, structured, made concrete, embodied, rendered visible. Here traditions, texts, persons, patterns of community and authority embody our sense of the sacred, mediate it to us, and facilitate our communion with it. Von Hügel's institutional element is roughly approximate to what people today mean when they speak of religion. Unfortunately, in the minds of many, religion is synonymous with rules, regulations, laws, structures, authority. The second element of religion is the intellectual. Here the formulation of cogent systems of thought and the development of our capacity for critical reflection help clarify our understanding of the sacred, communicate it to others, and serve to critique and strengthen ourselves and our communities when the gift and presence of the sacred in our midst is betrayed. The third element is what von Hügel calls the mystical element of religion. This is a way of speaking of the experience of the sacred, the dimension of spiritual life as experience. And this is closest to what is meant today when people speak of spirituality.

For von Hügel all three elements have a place. And the key is that there needs to be an interaction, a cross-pollination among the three. The institution must be attentive to the intellectual and mystical dimensions of the human quest for the sacred. But it is also true for von Hügel that the quest for the sacred must be related to a religious body in which texts, traditions, and communities communicate or mediate the presence of the sacred. And further, this mystical quest must attend to the rigorous intellectual element as well.

Now there is a sense in which von Hügel affirms the preeminence of the mystical element even while saying that all three must be held together in a noble tension. And so it is quite understandable that when people in search of a deep spirituality find themselves in religious institutions which are insipid, and alienated by theological reflection that does not nourish and challenge them, they will seek another path. But, if von Hügel's insights are correct, then there is also a problem when the spiritual quest is undertaken while turning away from that which a religious institution provides, and when the need for intellect and serious reflection is scorned in the name of simplicity and practicality, or the primacy of subjective experience. Given that many people have moved away from religious institutions today because they have been failed by them, it is nonetheless crucial to recognize that some expression of what von Hügel called the institutional and intellectual elements are to be integrated in the quest for the sacred. They are required, not simply desirable. And they are not incidental to personal integration.

Today there is a great emphasis on a holistic approach to spirituality and the quest for the sacred. Curiously, however, von Hügel had a far more holistic approach to the sacred than many of the gurus in contemporary spirituality. He recognized that authentic spiritual growth and development is not simply a matter of standing on one's own two feet, taking personal responsibility for one's own life, and adopting attitudes and disciplines to increase one's awareness of the sacred. While this is part of its concern, spirituality has just as much to do with participation in relationships with others in community and in wider social spheres. The search for the sacred is not something done alone. Our sense of the sacred is mediated through texts, traditions, communal arrangements which embody our sense of meaning, purpose, value. Institutions and traditions enshrine the highest values we perceive and make it possible to pursue them with others.

Further, the spiritual quest is not just about what works. The life of the spirit is not simply a pragmatic concern. When religious traditions and institutions betray the gift of the sacred they seek to mediate, it is the intellectual element of religion, constantly engaged in critical reflection, which serves as a burr in the saddle, challenging institutions and traditions, reminding them of their task to mediate the sacred. Von Hügel's insights provide a desperately needed check against our overly pragmatic approaches in spirituality, precisely because he insists on the importance of the intellectual, the reflective, the theoretical. These are the very dimensions of the human personality which our contemporaries are so quick to deprecate as they speed down the spirituality superhighway exhorting us: Keep it simple, stupid! Forget the theories! How does this cash out in practice?

Because we are not pure spirits in our spiritual quest, we need structure, tradition, community. Because we are not simply what we do, but are persons of mind and heart as well, we need to cultivate the intellect and our capacity for reflective awareness. It is to our peril that we rule out of our sense of the sacred the need for tradition, text, community, and authority, i.e., von Hügel's institutional dimension or "religion" as it is commonly understood today. And we persist in traveling down a dead-end alley if we consider the riches of the intellect and critical reflection to be nothing more than impractical and useless abstraction. Both of these elements are central to the spiritual quest. Both are sorely neglected in so many developments in spirituality today which tend to be overly subjective to the detriment of more objective and external considerations, as well as preoccupied with pragmatic results, with what is useful, what works. The result, as so many currents in contemporary spirituality manifest, is a highly individualized, indeed privatized approach to the sacred, devoid of any clear sense of belonging to a community, and a lack of a clear sense of critical social responsibility which any authentic awareness of the sacred demands.

CONCLUSION

This chapter has provided a bird's eye view of the "spirituality sprawl." In the most general sense of the term, "spirituality" refers to the deep desire of the human heart for personal integration in light of levels of reality not immediately apparent, as well as those experiences, events, and efforts which contribute to such integration. Much of what is referred to as "spirituality" today is related to a vague sense of the "sacred," but with no direct reference to God. That is to say that many expressions of spirituality are not explicitly religious in the common understanding of the term. But it is important to note that many religious people, indeed many Christians, are attracted to such spiritualities and find great sources of enrichment in them. In this chapter we have delineated those developments in spirituality which appear to be having the most appeal to and influence upon a specifically religious and Christian spirituality. Given the vast array of spiritualities today, there is need for great discretion in the face of them all. When it comes to addressing the deepest desires of the human heart, it is never simply a matter of personal tastes and pleasures. Not all expressions of spirituality are authentic. And not all of them do in fact lead to personal integration and the fullness of human flourishing.

■   *Notes to Chapter 1*   ■

1. For a helpful treatment of the dynamics of addiction and dysfunction, see Gerald May, *Addiction and Grace*. San Francisco: Harper & Row, 1988.

2. Phyllis A. Tickle, *Re-Discovering the Sacred: Spirituality in America*. New York: Crossroad, 1995.

3. See, for example, the work of John Dominic Crossan, Burton Mack, Marcus Borg and others associated with the "Jesus Seminar." For a thorough critique of their efforts see Luke Timothy Johnson, *The Real Jesus: The Misguided Quest for the Historical Jesus and the Truth of the Traditional Gospels*. San Francisco: Harper, 1995.

4. Tickle, p. 13.

5. Tickle, p. 16.

6. Tickle, p. 13.

7. Joann Wolski Conn, ed. *Women's Spirituality: Resources for Christian Development*. Mahwah, NJ: Paulist, 1986, Introduction, p. 3.

8. Ewert Cousins, "Preface to the Series." *Christian Spirituality*. Vol. I: *Origins to the Twelfth Century*. Bernard McGinn, et al., eds. New York: Crossroad, 1985, p. xiii.

9. John Macquarrie, *Paths in Spirituality*. New York: Harper and Row, 1972, pp. 40, 47.

10. Gordon S. Wakefield, *The Westminster Dictionary of Christian Spirituality*. Philadelphia: Westminster, 1983, p. v.

11. Edward Kinerk, "Toward a Method for the Study of Spirituality." *Review for Religious* 40 (1981), p. 6.

12. Raimundo Panikkar, *The Trinity and the Religious Experience of Man: Icon-Person-Mystery*. Maryknoll, NY: Orbis, 1973, p. 9.

13. Walter Principe, "Toward Defining Spirituality." *Studies in Religion/Sciences Religieuses* 12/2 (1983), p. 139.

14. Sandra M. Schneiders, "Spirituality in the Academy." *Theological Studies* 50/4 (1989), p. 684.

15. Sandra M. Schneiders, "Theology and Spirituality: Strangers, Rivals, or Partners." *Horizons* 13/2 (1986), p. 266.

16. Though I find Phyllis Tickle's analysis helpful on many counts, I disagree with her interpretation of the impact of the Holocaust on the faith of the Jews. Tickle maintains that the Holocaust of the Jews did not amount to a rupture between God and what really mattered for the Jews: "Only the Jews, coming out of the hideousness of their own cataclysm, survived 1945 with God and the sacred sharing the same space." p. 22. She overlooks the import of this event for non-Jews, as well as for many Jews who raised questions about the existence of God and the efficacy of God's action in the world because of the Holocaust. For example, see the work of Richard L. Rubenstein, especially his *After Auschwitz: History, Theology, and Contemporary Judaism*. 2nd ed. Baltimore: Johns Hopkins, 1992.

17. Ronald Rolheiser, *The Shattered Lantern: Rediscovering a Felt Presence of God*. New York: Crossroad, 1995. Though Rolheiser addresses the problems which North Americans face in living the spiritual life, his insights are applicable to those beyond North America.

18. The impact of the cultural climate on the life of those in religious vows in the United States today has been analyzed by David J. Nygren and Miriam D. Ukeritis in *The Future of Religious Orders in the United States: Transformation and Commitment*. Westport, CT: Praeger, 1993.

19. Wade Clark Roof, *A Generation of Seekers: The Spiritual Journeys of the Baby Boom Generation*. San Francisco: Harper, 1993. See "The 'Religious' and the 'Spiritual,'" pp. 76–79.

20. Friedrich von Hügel, *The Mystical Element of Religion as Studied in Saint Catherine of Genoa and Her Friends*. 2 vols. London: J. M. Dent & Sons, 1961.

■   *Chapter 1: For Further Reading*   ■

Jon Alexander, "What Do Recent Writers Mean By *Spirituality?*" *Spirituality Today* 32 (1980), pp. 247–256.

Ewert Cousins, gen. ed. *World Spirituality: An Encyclopedic History of the Religious Quest*. New York: Crossroad, 1985–. Three volumes of this monumental 25-volume series are devoted to Christian spirituality. See

Christian Spirituality I, II, III. Bernard McGinn, et al., eds. (vols. 16, 17, 18 of the series).

Ewert Cousins, "Spirituality: A Resource for Theology." *Proceedings of the Catholic Theological Society of America* 35 (1980), pp. 124–137.

Michael Downey, "Spiritual Writing, Contemporary" in *The New Dictionary of Catholic Spirituality*. Michael Downey, ed. Collegeville, MN: Liturgical Press, 1993, pp. 916–922.

Robert Hamma, "The Changing State of Spirituality: 1968 and 1993." *America* (November 27, 1993), pp. 8–10.

Bradley C. Hanson, ed. "What Is Spirituality?" Part One in *Modern Christian Spirituality: Methodological and Historical Essays*. American Academy of Religion Studies in Religion, no. 62. Atlanta: Scholars Press, 1990, pp. 13–61.

Donagh O'Shea, "Gaps and Glimpses." *Spirituality* 1 (1995), pp. 3–6.

Walter Principe, "Toward Defining Spirituality." *Studies in Religion/Sciences Religieuses* 12/2 (1983), pp. 127–141.

Ronald Rolheiser, *The Shattered Lantern: Rediscovering a Felt Presence of God*. New York: Crossroad, 1995.

Wade Clark Roof, *A Generation of Seekers: The Spiritual Journeys of the Baby Boom Generation*. San Francisco: Harper, 1993. See "The 'Religious' and the 'Spiritual,'" pp. 76–79.

Sandra M. Schneiders, "Spirituality in the Academy." *Theological Studies* 50/4 (1989), pp. 676–697.

Sandra M. Schneiders, "Theology and Spirituality: Strangers, Rivals, or Partners?" *Horizons* 13/2 (1986), pp. 253–274.

Philip Sheldrake, "What Is Spirituality?" in *Spirituality and History: Questions of Interpretation and Method*. New York: Crossroad, 1992, pp. 32–56.

Phyllis A. Tickle, *Re-Discovering the Sacred: Spirituality in America*. New York: Crossroad, 1995.

Friedrich von Hügel, *The Mystical Element of Religion as Studied in Saint Catherine of Genoa and Her Friends*. 2 vols. London: J. M. Dent & Sons, 1961.

CHAPTER 2

What Is Christian Spirituality?

A specifically Christian spirituality can provide a necessary check against some of the problems in many currents in spirituality today. As an antidote to the individualistic tendencies which underpin many recent developments in spirituality and which tend to breed narcissism, Christian spirituality is rooted in a sense of belonging to a people who together express their sense of the sacred through word, gesture, action, event, tradition, community. The presence of the sacred is mediated through persons, preeminently the person of Jesus Christ. As a consequence the spiritual quest has everything to do with being in right relationship with God and living out the sense of the sacred in relationship with others in the believing community and the wider human community. In the Christian scheme of things the spiritual quest is for the glory of God. But it is never undertaken alone. Its purpose or end is not self-improvement of the individual or the betterment of the group. More importantly, because Christian spirituality is rooted in the affirmation of a personal God who is active in history and human life, and present to all creation, human effort, hard work and productivity are all facilitated by God's presence and action. Whatever growth and development there may be in the spiritual life, it is by God's gift. Whatever the results or the "outcomes," they are because of God's grace. God's gift and grace do not yield to our criteria of assessment and will not conform to the logic of our pragmatic preoccupation.

Those who profess faith in Jesus Christ and follow him in discipleship, living in the presence and power of the Holy Spirit, are *ipso facto* living a Christian spirituality. In light of the spirituality sprawl surveyed in the first chapter, it may be helpful at this stage to bring two interrelated questions to the fore: Is there something distinctive about *Christian* spirituality? And, if so, what precisely *is* a specifically Christian spirituality?

Whatever may be said about the merits of a Christian spirituality, it must be recognized at the outset that those who live by Christ's Spirit must take their place alongside others who are searching for authentic human flourishing. In other words, Christian spirituality is one expression of the human spirit's striving to make good on life. Christians must be willing to be in a relationship of mutuality and dialogue with all those who are sincerely seeking to advance the truly human. From a Christian perspective, God's providential plan is for the fullness of human flourishing, the redemption of the whole world. The call of the Spirit of Christ is to be discerned wherever and whenever human beings are striving to promote authentic growth in knowledge, in freedom, and in loving relationship to others. And this often takes place on the part of those who have never heard the name of Christ, those of other religious traditions, those who disavow any religious conviction, and those who are indifferent to explicitly religious values or principles.

In the Roman Catholic Church there has been a groundswell of interest in spirituality, especially since the Second Vatican Council. But it is now more commonly recognized that serious interest in spirituality is not limited to Catholics. Previously thought of as a particularly Catholic concern, there is now widespread interest in spirituality among Christians of different traditions.

Interest in Christian spirituality is most apparent in the increasing number of persons enrolled in spirituality courses offered through institutes, seminaries, colleges, and universities. It is evident in the commitment to a deep and sustained prayer life on the part of Christians of all walks of life, and in the growing number of ordinary people in support/study groups and small base communities that help participants develop a more mature spirituality. Interest in retreats, spiritual direction and discernment has grown to such an extent that there are now professional organizations (e.g., Retreats International and Spiritual Directors International) that provide mutual support and encouragement for people involved in retreat work and in spiritual direction. This mounting interest, especially apparent since the Second Vatican Council, has been accompanied by an explosion of books and essays in the area of spirituality by religious publishers, to say nothing of secular publishing houses, considered in the first chapter.

The question about a distinctively Christian spirituality is best answered if set within the broader context treated in chapter 1. We have seen that spirituality broadly understood refers to the human quest for personal integration in light of levels of reality not immediately apparent. And we have acknowledged that this quest may be engaged in without any explicit reference to God. In such instances we are dealing with nonreligious spiritualities. When the quest involves an explicit reference to God or the divine, then the spirituality is religious. And when the ultimate values perceived and pursued are rooted in the God disclosed in Jesus Christ, through the power of the Holy Spirit active and present in the community of discipleship called the church, then we are speaking of a specifically Christian spirituality.

It is important to recognize that both religious and nonreligious spiritualities may or may not be authentic. And the same is true for Christian spirituality. Belief in God, or Christ, does not guarantee that the spirituality of a person or group is authentic. Indeed there are innumerable expressions of spirituality which, while appealing to the name of God, or Christ, are depersonalizing, dehumanizing, sometimes even demonic.

HUMAN BEING: SPIRIT IN THE WORLD

A helpful guide in charting out the contours of a specifically Christian spirituality within the context of the more common and universal striving for personal integration is Karl Rahner (1904–1984), one of the most significant Christian theologians of this century. Briefly, Rahner envisioned the gift and task of personal integration in terms of self-transcendence: giving oneself and finding oneself in the experience of knowledge, freedom, and love. Rahner recognized human experience as a locus of God's revealing self-disclosure.[1] Not only did Rahner develop a full-blown systematic theology based on this insight, but he also generated a distinctive spirituality and a method of reflecting on spiritual experience. Ordinarily treated as a systematic theologian, Rahner the spiritual theologian has been the focus of some of the work of several contemporary writers, notably Harvey Egan, Anne Carr, Annice Callahan, James Bacik, Robert Masson, and J. Norman King.[2]

In Rahner's view, human beings are *spirit* in the world. *Spirit* here "names" that dimension of the human person which is distinct from but not opposed to the material, i.e., the body. The person is properly understood as a unity, a whole, rather than as a hybrid of competing parts of body and soul, flesh and spirit, mind and matter. The spiritual dimension of the person describes the ability that human beings possess which enables them to transcend or break out beyond themselves and the limits of self-isolation, self-preoccupation, and self-absorption. This they do through the pursuit of knowledge, freedom, and love. The human spirit is that which is drawn to unfathomable mystery, which believers call God. And this capacity to be pulled and drawn into mystery abides within each and every human being, whether they are religious or not, baptized or not. As such, human beings are by nature spiritual. All human beings are spiritual insofar as all have the capacity to know and be known, to love and be loved, to be free and enable others to be free. Each one is spiritual insofar as each one is, by nature, drawn to mystery. The different ways of actualizing or realizing these capacities for knowledge, freedom, and love, the diverse ways of participating in mystery, make human persons the very unique and irreplaceable beings they are.

For Rahner, human life and activity, events and history, are capable of disclosing the presence and action of God, that is, God's grace. Indeed all these can communicate the very life of God, whose nature is to express and communicate love in and through creation, and above all through human beings. On this basis, Rahner is able to spell out a view of spirituality rooted in everyday life rather than in rare and extraordinary occurrences. The ordinary, the humdrum, the day-in-and-day-out, is shot through with occasions for encountering the unfathomable gracious mystery. Grace, God's revealing self-communication, is loose in the world.

Central to Rahner's view is the conviction that there is a compatibility between human nature and God's grace. The transformation that God's life brings about perfects human nature which, though tainted by sin, is still essentially good because created in the image of God. Taking this a step further, Rahner concludes that all creation, both human and nonhuman life, can be the locus for discerning the presence of God and for the transformation of human life and the world which God's grace brings about.

This is not to say that God and humans are the same. Nor does it imply that human beings and their activities are divine, or that they become God in the process of transformation by grace. In recognizing the connections and similarities in the relationship between God and the world, it must be accepted that whatever region of likeness there may be between God and the world, the region of unlikeness and discontinuity remains.

For Rahner, there is in every human being a desire to be in relation to God. This desire may be explicit, as in the case of religious people who name the unfathomable gracious mystery "God." Or it may be implicit, as in the case of nonreligious people, practical agnostics, and even atheists. In Rahner's view, the desire for God may be found even in those who overtly deny the existence of God. Created, finite, limited, and longing for fulfillment, the human being seeks that which is uncreated, eternal, unlimited, vast. Integration of body, mind, and soul takes place gradually in the pursuit of knowledge, freedom, and love which have their origin and end in the sacred, a Higher Power, the Unoriginate Origin, the reality believers call God. For Rahner, prayer and other disciplines ordinarily associated with the spiritual life are properly understood when viewed in light of this basic, common, and universal desire to be in relation with God. Different forms of prayer, fasting, almsgiving, and other types of spiritual discipline are expressions of the human desire to surrender completely to unfathomable mystery, to God, who is the source of knowledge, freedom, and love.

It is possible for human beings to express and communicate their response and relation, their surrender, to the invisible and eternal gracious mystery. But this is possible only because God has first initiated a relationship with humans in and through creation and history. When humans express and communicate their desire to be in relationship with the gracious mystery, God, their response is inclusive of the full range of human experience. Human communication with God occurs in and through the whole array of words, actions, objects, events, indeed each and every dimension of human life, not just prayer, asceticism, meditation, contemplation, and other explicitly spiritual practices.

In this view, then, spirituality refers to the ongoing realization or actualization of the human capacity to move beyond the self in knowledge, freedom, and love in and through relationship with others and with God. When this self-transcendence is motivated by and directed to relationship with the reality named God, however this be understood, then this spirituality may be said to be specifically religious. But it need not be so. This quest takes on a specifically religious dimension when the person's ultimate concern is God, or when the highest ideal is understood as presence to or union with God. It becomes specifically a Christian form of spirituality when it is actualized by the gift of the Holy Spirit which brings about a relationship with God in Jesus Christ and others in the community which bears his name and lives by Christ's Spirit.

Rahner's investigations enable us to see more clearly the meaning of the terms "spirit" and "spirituality" in light of which we can take a closer look at a specifically Christian spirituality. The "Spirit of God, Spirit of Christ" or "Holy Spirit" lies at the heart of all Christian spirituality and thus requires explanation for a fuller understanding of "Christian spirituality," and "Christian spiritualities."

THE SPIRIT OF GOD

In the Old Testament, the Spirit of God is associated with life and power. The Hebrew word *ruah* has as its root meaning breath and wind. In Israel's understanding, God acts in and through the Spirit to bring forth life and to sustain all that is. Everything that lives, moves, and breathes does so by the power which is God's Spirit. The Spirit is not viewed in opposition to nature, the body, or the material world. Rather, the Spirit of God is that which brings forth and re-creates them. But this re-creative action of the Spirit is always yet to be fully accomplished, and so the Old Testament perspective on the Spirit is notably future-oriented. The Spirit symbolizes God's redemptive power in creating and re-creating a world and a people. It bespeaks God's graciousness and power, and is given particular expression in one anointed to be God's servant through leadership or prophecy. It also finds concrete embodiment in the entire community of the redeemed people, anointed to God's service.

SPIRIT OF GOD, SPIRIT OF CHRIST: THE HOLY SPIRIT

From a New Testament perspective, the Spirit of God has been bestowed on all creation in and through the person of Jesus Christ, God's Anointed One. Jesus stands in the tradition of the prophets, but because of his unique relation to God and God's Spirit, he does not merely bear and bestow the Spirit. He is the embodiment or incarnation of that Spirit, which is mediated in and through his person. In and through him the Holy Spirit is definitively poured out, heralding a new creation, a new people wrought and redeemed by his life and power.

This life and power find culmination and fullness of expression in the paschal mystery of Jesus. In his suffering, death, and resurrection, the power of love, God's Spirit, is definitely disclosed, transforming even suffering and death into new life. The Crucified One lives. Jesus risen appears to his disciples, breathing and thereby giving to them the breath and power of life anew. Thus the fullness of the life and power of God's Spirit comes in and through Christ's paschal mystery, and entails living in Christ and by the gospel proclamation of salvation in and through his life, death, and resurrection.

The Spirit mediated through the person of Jesus brings to fullness God's purposes in ushering in a new creation, a renewed and redeemed people. Consequently, Jesus' entire existence is understood to have been brought about by God's Spirit. Thus the Spirit of God is the Spirit in and of Christ. Jesus is the way to true and authentic life, the one who gives God's Spirit in and through the gift of himself in self-sacrificial love. The Spirit which brings about God's new creation is most precisely and personally manifest as the Spirit of Christ.

From a New Testament perspective, the avant-garde of the new creation wrought in Christ is the community of disciples, baptized in his name and in the power of the Holy Spirit. Following the death and resurrection of Jesus, it is the community of disciples, the church, which forms his Body, living and breathing by the power of his Spirit. Christ's Spirit extends the salvific action and re-creative presence of Jesus by raising up a community of witness, faithful service, prayer and worship, holiness of life, and discernment of God's continuing self-disclosure in creation and in history.

Belonging to this Body requires a conversion of heart and of life. It entails a willingness to take part in the life and practice of this community, and to abide by the words and work of Jesus as expressed in the teaching of the community. It also calls for participation in the life of faith and worship of the community, especially fidelity to the breaking of the bread and the taking up of the cup in which Christ's mysteries are celebrated in memory and in hope.

Life in Christ Jesus through participation in the community of disciples is made possible by Christ's Spirit which empowers one to live a life of witness, steadfast courage in adversity, and service. Faith, hope, and love are the Spirit's premier gifts to those baptized into Christ's Body. And the Body, the church, flourishes through the manifold gifts of the Spirit which are manifest in the lives of those who confess the lordship of the crucified Christ through their lips as well as in all their affairs. The life and power of Christ's Spirit in the church are recognized in the gifts and harvest of the Spirit: love, joy, peace, patience, kindness, gentleness, fidelity, self-control. The absence of the Spirit is expressed in self-indulgence, self-preoccupation, divisiveness, wrangling, jealousy, lust, and envy (Galatians 5:18 ff).

There is, then, an organic unity in the Spirit between Christ and the church. The Spirit of God embodied in the person of Christ is mediated in time and space in and through the community of disciples, the church. Through the community of disciples, the

Incarnation continues. In Jesus, God's life and power are immutably disclosed. In the lives of the followers of Jesus known as the church, the life and power of God continue to be present in time and space. The Spirit as the presence of God throughout the ages is the condition for the possibility of all that is. This presence has found both image and abode in the history of Israel, in the life, ministry, passion, death, and resurrection of Jesus, and in those who confess him as Lord.

This presence, however, is not fixed or limited to these particular expressions. As the life and power without which nothing that is would be, the Spirit of God, God's presence throughout the ages, is loose in the world. Everything that lives and breathes does so by the creative act of God. But from the perspective of Christian spirituality, the way in which human life, history, and the world are renewed and transformed so as to be ever more fully the image and abode of God, is through the Spirit of God mediated in the words and work, the self-sacrificial love of Christ Jesus.

Thus, like the dove bearing the branch of an olive tree after the flood, the Spirit signals hope for a new creation, a new people sustained by God's fidelity to the promise. Like a flame of fire, the Spirit of God enlightens the mind and guides the heart, quickening all within its touch. Like the breath we draw almost imperceptibly at each moment, the Spirit stirs and inspires, letting life continue. And whether it is imaged as a gust, breeze, or whisper, the Spirit bespeaks God's abiding presence at the heart of all that lives.

UNDERSTANDING THE HOLY SPIRIT

Christological studies since the Second Vatican Council have contributed significantly to a deeper understanding of Christ and his mysteries. This is due in part to the effort to articulate views of Christ at once deeply rooted in the biblical tradition and, at the same time, appropriate to contemporary modes of being and perceiving. Earlier views of Christ that stressed his lordship and dominion, and which were expressed in such images as Christ the King are now complemented and enriched by understandings of Christ which accent the role of Jesus as the

Compassion of God or the Liberator of the poor and oppressed. Images of the Christ of the crusaders of different sorts throughout history are now giving way to Christ the black Nazarene and to the Christ of non-Western, nonwhite cultures. Similarly, contemporary studies of God, normally called Abba or Father in Christian tradition and theology, have resulted in fresh images of God. Due especially to the work of Christian feminist theologians, we can now draw from a rich fund of images which together manifest something of the reality of God and of human beings in relation to God. These images include God the Mother, Friend, and Lover, and the world and all creation as not external or extrinsic to God, but as God's own body.[3] Such developments are met with mixed reactions. The retrieval of feminine images of God, even though biblically based, is sometimes judged as jeopardizing the fundamental understanding of God which lies at the core of Christian faith. Others argue, more persuasively, that imaging God as both male and female is an expression of the long-standing theological affirmation that God is ultimately incomprehensible, neither male nor female, and beyond human categories of gender.[4]

One of the more important developments in the effort to present an understanding of God at once in keeping with the Christian tradition while addressing the needs and perceptions of our age is the theological effort to reconceive the doctrine of the Trinity as a very practical doctrine with radical consequences for Christian living.[5] Often viewed as the loftiest and most abstract Christian doctrine, the Trinity is altogether practical because it is the uniquely Christian way of speaking of God as a communion of persons, divine and human, in loving relation. This understanding of God gives rise to an approach to Christian life which emphasizes equality, reciprocity, mutuality between and among persons rooted in the trinitarian relations in which there is no subordination or inequality of persons.

The work of recovering multiple images of God and of Christ has not been accompanied by an equally strong effort in regard to understandings of the Holy Spirit. The task of reimaging the Holy Spirit has not received the same attention as the task of finding images of God and Christ appropriate for our time. Consequently, there is a dearth of images and symbols which effectively communicate the reality of the Holy Spirit which lies at the heart of what we call Christian spirituality. White doves descending and tongue-like flames of fire are in and of themselves inadequate to express the divine presence among us which we call the Holy Spirit, especially when considered alongside the rich panoply of images and appellations for God and for Christ which are being cultivated in the life of the churches today.

Such a recovery of images which leads to a deeper understanding of the Holy Spirit is crucially important because it is in and through the Holy Spirit that we first encounter the life of God. It is in the love, tenderness, and mercy of a parent's love that a child gains the first hint of the source of all love made manifest in the person of Jesus. It is this same love and presence animating the hearts of all human beings in diverse cultures throughout the world, inclining all toward the unfathomable mystery discerned wherever there are traces of goodness, of truth, of beauty. And it is this which prompts all in the human family, wherever they may position themselves vis-à-vis religious belief, to work for the increase of knowledge, freedom, and love. Most importantly, it is this Spirit by which those baptized into the Body of Christ live. It is in and through the Spirit that we participate in the trinitarian life. If it is true that Christian life is life in Christ, it is equally true that there is no life in Christ save in and through the presence and power of the Spirit. Christian spirituality is, therefore, impoverished to the degree that it lacks a rich array of images and symbols to "name" the life and breath of God which quickens all that lives, bringing it to the fullness of life, moving the whole of creation toward God, the one Jesus called Abba.

CHRISTIAN SPIRITUALITY

In earlier approaches to Christian life, spirituality was often associated with the interior life, the life of the soul, the life of the virtues, and the pursuit of perfection through their exercise. Often missing in such approaches was sufficient attention to the daily round, the importance of economic accountability, social responsibility, the demands of domestic and civil life, and the healthy integration of sexual desire and activity. The soul was often viewed as the higher realm, and the spiritual life was aimed at keeping it unsullied from worldly concerns such as the tedium of family life and domestic concerns, the burdens of ill health, and the weight of too much work. While the view of Christian life in the Spirit in early Christian centuries was inclusive of all dimensions of life, and the integration of each and every dimension of life through the presence and power of the Spirit was part and parcel of the Christian way of life, such an integrated and integrating view did not last. Spiritual concerns became more and more narrow over the course of Christian centuries.

The effects of this gradual narrowing of what "Christian spirituality" signifies are still felt in the years after the Second Vatican Council. But this increasingly restricted and restrictive view of spirituality, coupled with the wrongheaded understanding of the spiritual life as the life of perfection to which few (i.e., priests, nuns, monks, vowed religious) can earnestly aspire, was dealt a decisive blow, at least in principle, at Vatican Council II. Particularly in its "Dogmatic Constitution on the Church," the council affirmed that all the baptized are called to one and the same holiness (*Lumen Gentium*, chapter 5).

One of the consequences of this more inclusive approach to holiness, however, is that it often presents the opposite problem to the one which burdened the church in the generations prior to the council. If the pre-conciliar period was marked by a restrictive and elitist view of spirituality, the post-conciliar period has been characterized by a surge, indeed an explosion, of interest in spirituality of all sorts on the part of a wide array of people. And this swell of interest in spirituality has been accompanied by widespread uncertainty about the precise meaning of the term "Christian spirituality." In Christian circles the term "spirituality" is used nearly as frequently and with as much imprecision as a term closely related to it—"experience." And like the term "experience," spirituality is unavoidably ambiguous. But the term does not apply to anything and everything as one might be led to conclude from the proliferation of programs and institutes, journals and magazines, workshops and weekend courses, retreats and graduate degree programs in spirituality.

In this move from a restrictive to an inclusive understanding of spirituality, is there an identifiable referent or subject to which the term "Christian spirituality" applies?

Spirituality is a rich, multivalent reality with four strands or levels to which the term applies. At the first level, the term refers to that reality which is named in speaking of human being as spirit in the world. Such a description affirms that the spiritual is a fundamental dimension of human being. This first meaning of spirituality refers to "the intrinsic, self-transcending character of all human persons and everything that pertains to it, including, most importantly, the ways in which that perhaps infinitely malleable character is realized in everyday life situations."[6] As spirit in the world, the human person has the capacity to receive and transmit life, to be open to being, life, and relationship.

At the second level, the term refers to the experience which actualizes or realizes the human capacity to be in relation with another, others, and God. Experience here refers to "whatever enters into the actual living of...ongoing, integrating self-transcendence," and this includes the mystical, theological, ethical, psychological, political, and physical aspects of experience.[7]

At the third level the term refers to the formulation of insight about this lived reality. Such formulation may be expressed in writings such as the sacred scripture, theological writings in the Christian tradition, as well as the treatises on prayer like those beginning with Cyprian in the West and Origen in the East. But such insight is not limited to the written word. It is also formulated in popular wisdom, song, legend, and story. It may be expressed in the visual arts: painting, architecture, and sculpture. And it may be expressed in aural forms, such as liturgical or sacred music. Finally, it may find expression in other historical formulations such as popular devotions, and liturgical and religious dress.

At the fourth and final level, spirituality refers to the scholarly discipline which studies the experience of the Christian spiritual life, i.e., the spiritual life as an existential project. Christian spirituality is the quest for an ever-deepening integration through union with God in and through Jesus Christ by living in accord with the Holy Spirit. The scholarly discipline which studies this experience is increasingly referred to as "Christian spirituality," a field of studies with its own object of investigation, approaches, and methods.

These four levels may be summarized as follows. Spirituality refers to: 1) a fundamental dimension of human being; 2) the full range of human experience as it is brought to bear on the quest for integration through self-transcendence; 3) the expression of insights about this experience; 4) a disciplined study. In light of these four levels it is important to note that the spirituality of many people may be quite deep and vital without there being any explicit awareness of the third and fourth levels. Sometimes very simple persons, for example the mentally handicapped or little children, may have quite profound spiritual experiences even if they are unable to formulate an understanding of these experiences or articulate a theological or ethical position.

At the risk of oversimplification, a shorthand definition of this complex of elements provided by Joann Wolski Conn may be helpful. With attention to a specifically Christian spirituality she maintains "the term spirituality refers to both a lived experience and an academic discipline."[8] It one accepts this definition, however, it is important to realize that, ordinarily, there is an intermediate phase or level to which the term "Christian spirituality" also applies. Walter Principe maintains that the intermediate area between the lived experience and the formal study of the experience is one in which spiritual experience is articulated and formalized in some fashion. He maintains that this intermediate level of spirituality is the "formulation of a teaching about the lived reality, often under the influence of some outstanding spiritual person."[9] This formulation then gives rise and form to other spiritual experiences. For example, the spiritual experience of Ignatius Loyola is expressed and crystallized in the *Spiritual Exercises* and the *Constitutions* of the Society of Jesus. These writings have given rise to, and have been deeply formative of, the spiritual lives of generations of Jesuits and others who have lived an Ignatian apostolic spirituality. And these writings are themselves part of the data to be investigated by those who are interested in studying the experience of life in the Spirit on the part of Ignatius and his followers.

As a lived experience, Christian spirituality is a way of living for God in Christ through the presence and power of the Holy Spirit. As such it is greatly enriched by an appropriate understanding of the central Christian doctrine of the Trinity which lies at the foundation of Christian faith and practice. Just as the Second Vatican Council's affirmation that the eucharistic liturgy is the source and summit of Christian life has brought about deeper appreciation of the centrality of the eucharist in Christian life and spirituality ("Constitution on the Sacred Liturgy," *Sacrosanctum Concilium*, no. 10), so too there has been a deeper recognition that the central Christian mystery, the Trinity, with its far-reaching practical implications, constitutes the heart and soul of Christian spirituality.[10]

CHRISTIAN SPIRITUALITY IS TRINITARIAN SPIRITUALITY

Christian spirituality considered from this perspective is not anything other than Christian life in the Spirit: being conformed to the person of Christ, and being united in communion with God and with others. Because redemption through Jesus Christ and divinization through the Holy Spirit comprise the Christian life, any adequate understanding of Christian spirituality must be grounded in the mystery of the Trinity. The doctrine of the Trinity functions as the summary of Christian faith, expressing the central Christian conviction that the God who saves through Christ by the power of the Spirit lives eternally in a communion of persons, divine and human, in love.

The connection between the Trinity and the spiritual life has not always been clear, or clearly drawn. Because the Trinity has by and large been viewed as an abstraction since the fifth century, this eminently practical doctrine has lost its footing as the central and unifying Christian mystery. This has resulted in an impoverished Christian spirituality, as well as an understanding of God cut off from the wellsprings of spirituality. Current efforts to retrieve and rethink the mystery of the Trinity in light of the riches of the tradition and in view of contemporary insights and needs is required, not merely desirable, if an authentic and appropriate contemporary Christian spirituality is to flourish.

What is the doctrine of the Trinity at its heart, at its best? The doctrine of the Trinity affirms that it belongs to God's very nature to be committed to human beings and our history, that God's covenant with us is irrevocable, that God's face is immutably turned toward us in love, that God's presence to us is utterly reliable and constant. The basis for these affirmations is the self-revelation of God in salvation history, specifically, for Christians, in the self-communication of God in Jesus Christ. Christian living is the Spirit-assisted response to the Incarnate Word of God, Jesus Christ, who reveals the face of the invisible God.

Different images and metaphors have been used to depict the triune God, for example, source-river-stream, or memory-intellect-will, or lover-beloved-love. A more helpful image in the Christian tradition is communion (*koinonia*), which expresses the inherent diversity yet equality and interdependence of the divine persons, Father, Son, and Spirit.

A Christian spirituality rooted in the mystery of the Trinity emphasizes community rather than individuality. The goal of the spiritual life entails perfection of one's relationships with others, rather than an ever more pure gaze of the mind's eye on some eternal truth "out there" or in one's interior life. From this perspective, spirituality naturally connects with the ethical demands of the Christian life, which flourishes in the increase of communion among persons rather than personal sanctification rooted in an ever-deepening inner gaze. Spiritual disciplines such as almsgiving, abstinence, and fasting are aimed at purifying one's relationships and establishing rightly ordered relationships based on mutuality, equality, and reciprocity rather than on domination and submission of one race to another, one class to another, one sex to another, and so on. Such an approach to various practices of the spiritual life stands in marked contrast to those views which tended to overemphasize self-purification through self-denial, often resulting in an increase in self will and self-preoccupation and isolation.

Since Christian spirituality is not just a dimension of the Christian life, but *is* the Christian life itself lived in and through the presence and power of the Holy Spirit, it concerns absolutely every dimension of life: mind and body, intimacy and sexuality, work and leisure, economic accountability and political responsibility, domestic life and civic duty, the rising costs of health care, and the plight of the poor and wounded both at home and abroad. Absolutely every dimension of life is to be integrated and transformed by the presence and power of the Holy Spirit.

CHRISTIAN SPIRITUALITIES

Properly understood, spirituality is not merely an aspect of Christian life concerned with devotions, forms of prayer, fasting, and other disciplines. Spirituality refers to the whole of Christian life in response to the Spirit. Different responses to the presence and activity of the Holy Spirit give rise to different forms of life, different paths of integration, wholeness, holiness. These may be recognized as diverse spiritualities. The various elements of spirituality such as prayer, meditation, contemplation, and asceticism, are properly understood as means of response to the Spirit, that is, means of bringing about ever fuller participation in the life of God and God's providential plan for creation.

The whole history of Christian spirituality may be viewed as the ongoing quest for personal integration through self-transcendence in pursuit of the highest ideals and ultimate values perceived by persons and communities. Various figures and movements in Christian history have attended to this task in quite different ways. In other words, ultimate values and highest ideals have been perceived and pursued in different ways by different individuals and groups. And so there are diverse understandings of prayer, the importance of discernment of spirits, the function of a community, the need for a rule of life, and so on. There exists a panoply of approaches, different types and schools of spirituality, precisely because ultimate values and ideals have been and continue to be perceived and pursued in remarkably different ways.

All of these ways share some common features which are characteristic of any spirituality which is explicitly Christian. A Christian spirituality is rooted in the person of Jesus Christ and his word and work, especially as revealed in the scriptures, specifically the New Testament. Its hallmarks are faith, hope, and, above all, love. History demonstrates that individuals and groups give expression to these common features in a multiplicity of forms, however. They live the gospel differently because certain values and ideals which it discloses are perceived as more central than others in the task of self-transcendence and personal integration.

A diversity of Christian spiritualities flourished in different forms of life motivated by the gospel message during what is sometimes referred to as the evangelical awakening of the High Middle Ages. This period was characterized by the emergence of pluriform patterns of living the gospel more intensely. It must be recognized that attention to the Incarnate Word of God as mediated in the gospel text has not always been given the same priority in every period of Christian history as it was in the evangelical awakening of the Middle Ages. In this light, one can better appreciate the singularly important role the gospel text itself played for the medieval Christian and how it revealed the Incarnate Word in the humanity of Jesus.

But the Word as focus of self-transcendence and personal integration was perceived in very different ways and pursued down different paths. The Cistercians approached Christ the Incarnate Word by focusing upon his humanity, striving for union with God through the heart of Christ. The Word is touched, indeed tasted, by an affective embrace in which love's kiss is exchanged. The approach to the Word which characterizes the Victorines Richard and Hugh differs considerably. Here the ideal is to give expression to the Word through example which edifies the community. The Word is thereby efficacious. Others, like Alan of Lille, viewed the ideal in terms of public preaching of the Word so that it might lead others to embrace the fullness of Christian life. For Francis of Assisi it was by literal imitation of the life of Christ in the gospel that the ideal of the Word was to be achieved. And for Dominic and his followers, the ultimate value of the Word was actualized in the public preaching of the Word in response to the need of the faithful for sound exposition of Christian truth in the face of aberrations.

Though all of these individuals and movements attend to the value and ideal of the Word of God in the task of self-transcendence in relation to another, others, and God, the particular approach to and appropriation of the Word in each gives rise to a distinct Christian spirituality, a different approach to living the message of the gospel.

Similarly, in the present day there are quite diverse Christian spiritualities resulting from the way in which the highest ideal or ultimate value is perceived and pursued. Under the inspiration of Dorothy Day, those committed to the Catholic Worker Movement strive for the ideal of a Christianly inspired community of peace and justice through serving the needs of the poor and the disen-franchised, and by means of efforts to build a world in which all may grow. The ideal of loving service of the Christ who hungers and thirsts in the poorest of the poor is pursued by Mother Teresa of Calcutta and the Missionaries of Charity through the work of compassionate presence to those who are most neglected and abandoned in our world. The value of unity between and among Christians is pursued in the praxis of forgiveness and reconcilia-tion in the communities of Taizé and of Grandchamp, two monastic communities of men and of women respectively, which count in their number members of the various divided Christian denominations and churches. The value of the dignity and sacredness of the human person, even and especially the most severely and profoundly mentally handicapped, leads Jean Vanier and the communities of l'Arche to live together in communities inspired by the beatitudes, wherein the poor and the wounded hold pride of place, and the weak and vulnerable are the teachers of the clever and the strong. And the followers of the Rule of Benedict pursue the ideal of listening for God in the rhythms of work and prayer throughout the day. Those who live in the Ignatian tradition pursue the ideal of finding God in all things. Consequently they engage in a wide scope of activities, all of which are to be accomplished in a disposition of service while striving for excellence for the greater glory of God.

Thus there exists a great variety of Christian spiritualities both past and present. They arise from different ways of perceiving and pursuing the highest ideals and ultimate values disclosed in and through Christ Jesus. But the question remains: How does one account for these different perceptions of value and diverse approaches to realizing or actualizing the highest ideal? Why is it that the perceptions differ and the pursuit is so varied?

If human beings are spirit in the world, then the specific world in which they live will color their perceptions. And this world in which human beings exist influences more than just the interior life or the life of perfection. Therefore it is necessary to be mind-ful of the much wider context within which the human quest for self-transcendence is actualized and in which the Holy Spirit is at work in manifold ways.

CONCLUSION

In this chapter, some of the key terms of the vocabulary of spirituality have been defined in view of the concern to answer the question: What is Christian spirituality? We have seen that Christian spirituality refers most fundamentally to living the Christian life in and through the presence and power of the Holy Spirit. Christian spirituality is most profitably understood when viewed in the context of the more basic and fundamental human quest for integration of mind, body, and soul. The thought of Karl Rahner is helpful in this regard, precisely because he views Christian life in the Spirit as a particular, indeed unique, expression of the universal human desire for integration and completion through self-transcending knowledge, freedom, and love.

Christians have sought to live by the presence and power of the Holy Spirit throughout history. And this they have done in a breathstopping variety of ways. When faced with the sprawl of contemporary spirituality, viewing the Christian tradition can provide helpful insights for the task of recognizing authentic expressions of spirituality in our own day. Indeed, to live a Christian spirituality today requires some conscious relationship to its traditions. But how the Christian tradition is to be viewed, and just how contemporary Christians are to relate to it, is an issue which has found no final resolution. To this we now turn.

■ *Notes to Chapter 2* ■

1. A compendium of Rahner's spirituality is available in English under the title *The Practice of Faith: A Handbook of Contemporary Spirituality.* New York: Crossroad, 1983. See also his foundational works: *Spirit in the World*, New York: Continuum, 1994; *Hearer of the Word*, New York: Continuum, 1994.

2. See Harvey D. Egan, "'The Devout Christian of the Future Will...be a "Mystic".' Mysticism and Karl Rahner's Theology" in *Theology and Discovery: Essays in Honor of Karl Rahner, S.J.* William J. Kelly, ed. Milwaukee: Marquette University Press, 1980, pp. 139–158; Anne E. Carr, *Transforming Grace: Christian Tradition and Women's Experience.* San Francisco: Harper & Row, 1988; Annice Callahan, *Karl Rahner's Spirituality of the Pierced Heart: A Reinterpretation of Devotion to the Sacred Heart.* Lanham, MD: University Press of America, 1985; James J. Bacik, *Apologetics and the Eclipse of Mystery: Mystagogy According to Karl Rahner.* Notre Dame, IN: University of Notre Dame Press, 1980; Robert Masson, "Spirituality for the Head, Heart, Hands, and Feet: Karl Rahner's Legacy." *Spirituality Today* 36 (1984), pp. 340–354; J. Norman King, "The Experience of God in the Theology of Karl Rahner." *Thought* 53 (1978), pp. 174–202; J. Norman King, *Experiencing God All Ways and Every Day.* Minneapolis: Winston Press, 1982; James A. Wiseman, "'I Have Experienced God': Religious Experience in the Theology of Karl Rahner." *The American Benedictine Review* 44 (1993), pp. 22–57.

3. See the work of Sallie McFague, *Metaphorical Theology: Models of God in Religious Language.* Philadelphia: Fortress, 1982; *Models of God: Theology for an Ecological, Nuclear Age.* Philadephia: Fortress, 1987; *The Body of God: An Ecological Theology.* Minneapolis: Fortress, 1993.

4. A fine example of this is the work of Elizabeth A. Johnson, *She Who Is: The Mystery of God in Feminist Theological Discourse.* New York: Crossroad, 1992. See also Elizabeth A. Johnson, "The Incomprehensibility of God and the Image of God Male and Female." *Theological Studies* 45 (1984), pp. 441–465.

5. The best example of a recovery and reconceptualization of the doctrine of the Trinity is Catherine Mowry LaCugna, *God for Us: The Trinity and Christian Life.* San Francisco: Harper, 1991. See also Colin Gunton, *The Promise of Trinitarian Theology.* Edinburgh: T. & T. Clark, 1993; Ted Peters, *God as Trinity: Relationality and Temporality in the Divine Life.* Louisville, KY: Westminster/John Knox, 1993.

6. Richard Woods, *Christian Spirituality: God's Presence Through the Ages*. Chicago: Thomas More, 1989, p. 3; rev. ed. Allen, TX: Christian Classics/ Thomas More, 1996.

7. Sandra M. Schneiders, "Theology and Spirituality: Strangers, Rivals, or Partners." *Horizons* 13/2 (1986), p. 267.

8. Joann Wolski Conn, "Spirituality" in *The New Dictionary of Theology*. Joseph A. Komonchak, et al., eds. Wilmington, DE: Michael Glazier, 1987, p. 972.

9. Walter Principe, "Toward Defining Spirituality." *Sciences Religieuses/ Studies in Religion* 12/2 (1983), p. 136.

10. Catherine Mowry LaCugna, *God for Us*; Catherine Mowry LaCugna and Michael Downey, "Trinitarian Spirituality" in *The New Dictionary of Catholic Spirituality*. Michael Downey, ed. Collegeville, MN: Liturgical Press, 1993, pp. 968–992.

■ *Chapter 2: For Further Reading* ■

Christian Spirituality I, II, III (vols. 16, 17, 18 of *World Spirituality*. Ewert Cousins, gen. ed.). Introductions to the 3 vols. New York: Crossroad, 1986–1991.

Harvey D. Egan, "The Mysticism of Everyday Life." *Studies in Formative Spirituality* 10/1 (1989), pp. 7–26.

Richard Hardy, "Christian Spirituality Today: Notes on Its Meaning." *Spiritual Life* 28/3 (1982), pp. 151–159.

Cheslyn Jones, Geoffrey Wainwright, and Edward Yarnold, eds. Introduction. *The Study of Spirituality*. Oxford; New York: Oxford University Press, 1986.

Jean Leclercq, Introduction. *The Spirituality of Western Christendom*. E. Rozanne Elder, ed. Kalamazoo, MI: Cistercian Publications, 1976.

Walter Principe, "Spirituality, Christian" in *The New Dictionary of Catholic Spirituality*. Michael Downey, ed. Collegeville, MN: Liturgical Press, 1993, pp. 931–938.

Karl Rahner, *Encounters with Silence*. James M. Demske, trans. Westminster, MD: Newman Press, 1960.

Karl Rahner, "Experience of the Holy Spirit." *Theological Investigations* Vol. 18, pp. 189–210.

Karl Rahner, "Experience of Self and Experience of God." *Theological Investigations* Vol. 13, pp. 122–132.

Karl Rahner. Foreword. *Theological Investigations* Vol. 16.

Karl Rahner, "Is Prayer Dialogue with God?" in *Christian at the Crossroads*. New York: Seabury/Crossroad, 1975, pp. 62–69.

Karl Rahner, "Mystical Experience and Mystical Theology." *Theological Investigations* Vol. 17, pp. 90–99.

Karl Rahner, "Reflections on the Experience of Grace." *Theological Investigations* Vol. 3, pp. 86–90.

Karl Rahner, "Religious Enthusiasm and the Experience of Grace." *Theological Investigations* Vol. 16, pp. 35–51.

Karl Rahner, *Visions and Prophecies*. Vol. 10 of *Quaestiones Disputatae*. New York: Herder and Herder, 1964.

Frank Senn, ed., *Protestant Spiritual Traditions*. Mahwah, NJ: Paulist, 1986.

Philip Sheldrake, *Spirituality and History: Questions of Interpretation and Method*. New York: Crossroad, 1992.

"Spiritualité" and related articles in *Dictionnaire de spiritualité ascétique et mystique. Doctrine et histoire*. M. Viller, F. Cavallera, and J. de Guibert, eds. Paris: Beauchesne, 1932–1995.

"Spirituality" and related articles in *New Catholic Encyclopedia*. Washington, DC: Catholic University of America, 1967– .

Gordon S. Wakefield, "Spirituality" in *Westminster Dictionary of Christian Spirituality*. Gordon S. Wakefield, ed. Philadelphia: Westminster, 1983.

CHAPTER 3

A Living Tradition

Why is there such a strong interest in the traditions of Christian spirituality today? Why are people reading the spiritual writers of the past in ever-increasing numbers? No one answer to this question is adequate in light of the complexity of the issue. But it may be useful to consider that in periods of cultural upheaval and disorientation such as ours, there often emerges a deep appreciation for the merits of earlier periods of history. This interest can be naive and romantic fascination. Too frequently, a bygone era is viewed as a golden age which can quickly become a golden calf. My mother's homespun Irish wisdom is sobering: "The good old days were good except for those who had to live through them!"

At this juncture of our history, we often feel that the world is coming apart at the seams. Oftentimes it appears that we are left without a compass while on a journey. Many seem to have lost their way altogether. Indeed, the metaphor of the spiritual life as a journey, which implies that there is a point of destination, is itself subject to scrutiny. Is the journey any longer a fitting description of the Christian way of life?

Sometimes it seems that we are standing in the midst of ruins: cultural, social, political, and religious. Consider the violence inflicted upon innocent millions, the massacre of whole races of people, the aggression of powerful races against the defenseless, the generations-old conflict in Northern Ireland, the horror of the AIDS epidemic, the banality of senseless crime, the obscenity of gangsta rap music, the slaughter of hundreds of thousands in a war among the peoples of Rwanda and of Bosnia. All these events baffle and disorient. The interruption of our worlds of meaning and order brought on by the shock of events, the terror of history, calls into question the tightly knit belief in a divine plan and a provident God. We are overwhelmed with a sense of chaos. This cultural, social, political, and religious breakdown has an impact upon every dimension of life. Whole worlds of meaning and purpose and value are in shambles. Much of what made the world seem so secure and reliable has been shattered. We lack the sense of unity, clarity, and security that earlier generations could count on.

In light of this overwhelming sense of fragmentation shared by so many, there is a growing awareness of the need to rely on hidden reserves, inner strength, the life of the spirit in the human heart. As outer worlds of meaning collapse, there seems to be a movement inward. And in the hope of finding companions and guides for the spiritual life, we find ourselves turning to those who have gone before us.

TURNING TO HISTORY AND TRADITION

Christian spirituality is necessarily related to the Christian tradition. Those who seek to live in and through the Spirit recognize that they are part of an ongoing story with roots long, deep, and strong. This needs to be affirmed all the more these days when the risks of "presentism" are very high. Many people today are unable to see any value whatsoever in the ways and wisdom of long ago. For far too many the past is old-fashioned, and newer is necessarily better. Such a view, under the guise of being modern and progressive, is shortsighted and arrogant.

Especially since the Second Vatican Council, there has been a turn to history, a return to the sources of Christian faith and life, a deeper historical consciousness, and a recognition of the importance of understanding spiritual figures and movements in light of the context in which they lived in Christ by the presence and power of the Spirit. With this has come a clearer recognition of the strengths of the tradition and of the ways in which its collective spiritual wisdom can enrich contemporary life. But there is also an awareness that the tradition's spiritual wisdom has its shortcomings too. It cannot provide ready answers as we face some of the pressing problems of our own day.

Persons such as Teresa of Avila and John of the Cross, the Beguines, Meister Eckhart, Francis and Clare of Assisi, Mechtild of Magdeburg, Hildegard of Bingen, Bernard of Clairvaux, and Charles de Foucauld attract considerable attention among contemporary Christians. The interest in spiritual figures and movements of earlier epochs has found expression and further impetus in the great number of publications in our own century, many of which are particularly attentive to the history of Christian spirituality. Art, architecture, music, vesture, and a wide range of other nonliterary expressions from the expansive history of Christian spirituality, along with the burgeoning number of publications in the area of spirituality, make the rich and varied spiritual traditions of Christianity more widely available to contemporary Christians. Any survey of these publications is indicative of the great longing for deeper familiarity with those who have gone before us in the life of the Spirit.[1]

LOOKING TO THE PAST: TAKING DIFFERENT DIRECTIONS

The turn toward tradition and history to find therein great riches for the spiritual life is a great strength and a welcome development. However, it must be recognized that contemporary Christians turn to the past for quite different reasons. At the risk of oversimplification, it may be helpful to suggest that there are at root two ways of viewing the past, both of which are prevalent today. Both merit attention here. The first might be best understood in light of the image of "seeking refuge," the second in light of "retrieving riches."

Whatever else may have been changed by the Second Vatican Council, it has not altered the fact that people in great numbers continue to read Thomas à Kempis' *Imitation of Christ*, Thérèse of Lisieux's *Story of a Soul*, Butler's *Lives of the Saints,* and similar favorites of the spiritual life. Many remain deeply committed to their devotions and novenas and practices of piety. They carry prayer cards and request Masses for their dead. They pray the rosary and wear Miraculous Medals. Some display medals and small statues of Saint Christopher in their cars even as they lament his absence on the revised liturgical calendar. Many still wear scapulars of all kinds, and heartily welcome Fulton Sheen into their living rooms via VCR. But the motivations for continuing with such practices of popular piety, which seem more typical of an earlier period of history, are quite varied.

SEEKING REFUGE IN TRADITION

Given the social and cultural upheaval we face, it is not at all surprising to find that increasing numbers turn to the past because they see in the days gone by a haven of solace and security. There is among many a strongly held conviction that the Second Vatican Council was a wrong turn in the church's history. There are those who lament many of the changes in the church and want to return to the way things were. There is a deep longing for "traditional" spirituality, though what people are usually referring to by this term is a form of spirituality which prevailed in the 19th century. Such traditional spirituality is hardly representative of the rich spiritual traditions of Christianity.

This manner of looking at the past is usually spurred on by a profound sense of being beleaguered by the dechristianization of the contemporary world, a conviction that the world is "going to hell in a handbasket." And so there is an earnest desire to get back to a more authentic form of faith and spiritual life. It is often expressed through reading stories about Padre Pio, books by Louis Grignion de Montfort, stories about Bernadette of Lourdes, the apparition at LaSalette, legends of miracles, the poem of the Man-God by Maria Valtorta, fascination with apparitions at Medjugorje and with the secrets of Our Lady of Fatima. If the truth be told, the finger-wagging Mother Angelica and her team of televangelists are representative of the religious and spiritual sensibilities of a considerable number of contemporary Catholics who view tradition and history in such a way.

Whatever merits the practices of this so-called traditional spirituality may have, some of them are rooted in apocryphal sources. Many of these currents are expressions of a new Catholic fundamentalism. It is difficult to pin down a precise definition of Catholic fundamentalism, but it is succinctly expressed in the sentiment: "Whatever is going on in today's world, we don't much like it. We'd rather have it the way it was." Among Catholic fundamentalists there is fascination with "old time religion," an admiration for dogmatic televangelists who give clear and precise answers to highly complex issues with which people are struggling in today's world. In this cast of mind, the contemporary world is depraved, debauched, and decadent. Refuge is therefore sought in a church with clear boundaries which guarantees salvation, within a tradition which is understood to be essentially unchanging. The function of spirituality here is to provide a buffer, a "comfort zone" of refuge while living in this vale of tears. Such an approach to spirituality cultivates mounting fascination with apparitions, weeping statues, special revelations, messages of gloom and impending doom. Along these same lines there is a preoccupation with the full range of extraordinary phenomena that have little or nothing to do with the ordinary challenges that must be faced by most Christians in a highly complex world.

These tendencies are not found only among Catholics, as a quick exercise in "channel surfing" will go to show. Indeed the majority of Christian televangelists are non-Catholic. The efforts of these traditionalists are more often than not promoted by upscale, state of the art, high technology. Followers are exhorted to return to a spirituality of a bygone era. Among the most traditionalist and conservative of voices, there is a bold defiance in the face of those ardently seeking to grapple with pressing contemporary issues and concerns. And there is a righteousness, indeed arrogance, which is expressed in the insistence that all the problems we face would be solved if we would return to the way it used to be. Such traditionalist tendencies are endorsed and reinforced by political forces and strengthened by the wealth of religious and political conservatives who are ordinarily resistant to any sort of change whatsoever.

Without doubt, the traditionalist approach to the traditions of Christian spirituality has some merit. But it must be recognized that, even in its most favorable expressions, the spiritual tradition

which prevailed prior to the Second Vatican Council and to which
the traditionalists exhort us to return, had several shortcomings.
A few of these are worthy of note here.[2]

First, the spirituality of past generations tended to be theoretical in its starting point and presuppositions. Said another way, in
many former approaches there was little if any attention to
human experience as the very "stuff" of spirituality, the point of
entry in the spiritual life. Approaches to the spiritual life began
with airtight concepts and tightly knit doctrines of grace and sin,
precise rules for various approaches to prayer, and clearly
defined methods of prayer which one would follow rigorously as
an expression of one's sincerity in growing in the spiritual life. In
such an approach there was little room for diversity of personality, for real differences between and among persons based on
sex, race, social standing, state in life, economic and educational
background, and so on. Theories of the spiritual life were
applied willy-nilly to any and all interested in spirituality.

Second, the spirituality of previous ages was often elitist in its
assumptions. Priests and religious, monks and nuns, were looked
upon as those who were called to the higher regions of the spiritual life. They had a "vocation." Laypersons who took the spiritual life seriously were sometimes referred to as "missed
vocations." Children who expressed interest in religion or the life
of faith were looked upon as "potential vocations." By implica-
tion, laypersons were not called. Marriage, though understood as
a sacramental reality was, in practice, treated as an obstacle or a
handicap to be overcome if one would live an authentic spiritual
life. Indeed life in the world was judged inferior to the lives of
those who left the world to pursue a higher calling. The net
effect of this approach is that the centrality of baptism by which
all are called to life in Christ was eclipsed. And the nature of the
church as a sacrament in and to the world was unwittingly
neglected in the process of urging persons serious about the spiritual life to leave the world so that their lives could be given to
the church.

Third, the spirituality passed down from previous epochs
tended to be otherworldly. With a strong dose of asceticism, the
spiritual life was thought to consist, in the main, of sacrifices
and acts of self-denial and self-abnegation. Life in this world was

looked upon as somewhat incidental in view of the everlasting joys of heaven. This had the effect of inculcating a sense of arrogance toward those who had to face the daily task of life in this world: feeding and clothing children, education, civic duty, economic accountability, political responsibility. Even in its better forms, this spirituality tended to cultivate a sense of indifference with regard to the complex issues and urgent demands which people in the world must confront in every age. It also had the effect of allowing for an unhealthy measure of indifference in relation to the plight of the vast number of those who are poor and who suffer. In shunning their responsibility for life in the world and for the lives of others, many consoled themselves in the facile belief that eternal life is the only life that really matters.

Above all, the traditionalist approach to the spiritual life was (and remains) highly individualistic. Rosemary Haughton's comments are instructive here:

> The spirituality we inherited, for all the richness and holiness it bred, is essentially for the individual....This spirituality puts the full responsibility for the search for God and for holiness on the person, though he or she is expected to need direction, and probably the structure of a life specifically designed to support spiritual search. The goal of human life is perceived as personal salvation and if possible holiness, so that even the traditional and energetic Christian commitment to the service of people in need is interpreted as a means to the holiness of the person who serves.[3]

The purpose in noting these shortcomings is not to urge that the tradition of Christian spirituality be jettisoned. Nor is it to argue that newer is better, older is old-fashioned. Even with these and other shortcomings, there is much in the tradition that can profit Christians for living in today's world. But profit will be gained from the *long* tradition of Christian spirituality, which calls for a careful and critical retrieval of this rich reserve of wisdom.

RECOVERING RICHES OF THE TRADITION

A second way of looking to history pays close attention to the past in search of riches which can enhance life in the Spirit in today's world. Such a perspective recognizes that the past has both gems and rubble, and that these must be sifted through in an effort to profit from the riches of the past. To recover some of the tradition's wealth, it may be useful to survey the way in which the term "spirituality" has been used in Christian history. Such a survey will show how early Christian understandings of spirituality, which were by and large holistic and integrated, gradually became more and more narrow. Such a survey will also indicate that the theoretical, elitist, otherworldly, and individualistic understandings which came to be our inherited spirituality prior to the Second Vatican Council are not to be equated with an authentic traditional spirituality. Indeed, there are much earlier understandings which provide the basis for the renewed vision of Christian life which was heralded by the Second Vatican Council.

LEARNING FROM HISTORY

In view of the long history of the Christian tradition, the term "spirituality" is itself of rather recent vintage.[4] Its roots lie in the Pauline term "spiritual" (*pneumatikos*), the adjectival form of the Greek term for Holy Spirit (*pneuma*). The term "spiritual" was used by Paul to describe any reality which was under the sway of the Holy Spirit. In particular, he used the term to describe the "spiritual" person in contrast to the "natural" person (1 Cor 2:14–15). What is important to note here is that Paul is not describing the spiritual dimension of the person, or the soul as an invisible and intangible reality, in contrast to the material dimension or the body of the person. Rather, he is distinguishing the person as a unified being who is moved by the presence and action of the Holy Spirit, in contradistinction to the person unaided by this gift.

This understanding perdured for the most part throughout Christian history until the 12th century, navigating its way through the terrain of various types of dualism, perhaps most notably that of Manichaeism and its different manifestations. Due to philosophical developments which influenced theology in the Middle Ages, there emerged an understanding of the spiritual which placed it in opposition to the material. Though the person was still viewed as a unified being, and was not yet understood as a composite being made up of separate faculties of intellect and will, reason and emotion, or of separate sides or parts of body and soul, matter and spirit, these distinctions were clearly drawn in the High Middle Ages, paving the way for later generations to draw the line much too sharply.

By the 17th century, particularly in France, "spiritual" and "spirituality" came to refer to the interior life, bearing strong affective connotations. This must be understood in light of the affirmation, often made during this period, that the will is superior to the intellect by virtue of its proper end. The result is a sharp cleavage unknown in the High Middle Ages, but foreshadowed in some influential theological writings, notably those of Jean Gerson (b. 1363). It is perhaps with Gerson that the split between spirituality and other dimensions of Christian life and practice, especially theological reflection, begins with unfortunate consequences even into the 20th century. Gerson untethered what we would now call spirituality from theological reflection on the grounds that there is a different object or end for each. He argued that while the object of the spiritual approach is union with God perceived as ultimate Goodness, the object of the theological approach is union with God perceived as ultimate Truth.[5]

One unfortunate result of this separation is that later generations came to be suspicious of spirituality as something irrational, enthusiastic, unbridled, and often unorthodox. Thus the term began to bear quite negative significance. For example, in 17th century France, "spirituality" was used in contradistinction to the term "devotion," the latter referring to a more balanced and sober approach to Christian life and practice. It is in 17th-century France that we find the strongest precedent for the pre-Vatican II understanding of spirituality as pertaining to the interior life, the life of perfection, to which few are called by nature or by grace. No longer does the term "spirituality" refer to the life of the Spirit given by incorporation into Christ's Body, the church, through the sacraments of initiation and ongoing participation in the eucharist. Rather, it is the prerogative of the few, mostly clergy and religious. By exception, people in the world may be introduced to the devout life, but this often was understood as an extension of, or by comparison to, what was judged to lie within the precincts to which clergy and religious had access by virtue of their higher calling.

In the 18th and 19th centuries, "spiritual" and "spirituality" came to refer more and more to practices of Christian life and prayer in which the great majority of ordinary Christians were not engaged. "Spirituality" described the domain of the life of perfection and mystical graces which only some pursued. Thus, the spiritual life was not viewed as part and parcel of the baptismal vocation. It pertained to the life of interiority and perfection, as well as the life of mystical grace and union, which were all well beyond what was deemed necessary for authentic Christian life: adherence to the commandments, participation in the sacramental life, observance of tradition, and obedience to church teaching.

In the 19th century, spirituality took on a more practical and experiential emphasis, but this usually amounted to little more than implementing theological doctrines in the practical realm of Christian living. This was best accomplished by attention to the interior life of the individual who, only in some cases, was guided through the higher stages of Christian life, often by a spiritual director or directress who would oversee the spiritual exercises of the individual and assure that the insights gained by living the interior life were at once theologically orthodox and in harmony with what was already known to be virtuous by the canons of moral theology.

This brief survey reveals that understandings of spirituality are constantly in flux, and that there are different views of spirituality at different historical periods. What this helps us to recognize is that our view of the history of spirituality, what it is and what it offers, depends in large part on where we stand and how we view this history.

Most views of history tend to see it as a linear progression of a fixed insight, truth, or other reality which develops throughout the course of history but remains essentially unchanged from generation to generation. This is all too apparent in common understandings of the origins of the church. In such views, the church was founded by Jesus, and developed organically over time in a straight historical line, remaining essentially unchanged throughout. Careful historical and theological studies have shown that this is far too facile a reading of the very complex processes of the church's life. Recent historical studies demonstrate that historical development is not nearly so neat and tidy a process as some would like to suggest. This is true of the history of spirituality as well, though some very recent studies still hold out for the straightforward linear progressive view of its development.[6] Such approaches trace the development of Christian spirituality from biblical origins, through the Patristic period, the Middle Ages, the Reformation, the Modern period, and the contemporary period. Here the constant concern is to find threads which bind the history of spirituality together. But with this issue constantly to the fore, the sometimes unwieldy character of history is given short shrift. Not nearly enough room is allowed for the rich and varied experiences of the spiritual life which are to be uncovered from the tradition.

Other recent studies of spirituality which attend to alternative experiences, not just the mainstream of history, are more instructive and suggest that the nature of history itself defies neat linear development. Indeed, history is more sporadic, episodic, indeed seemingly random. History challenges the notion of a tidy unfolding of some preordained plan, even if the realities in question are "spiritual." History is riddled through and through with those smack-in-the-face unsettling events and experiences that call into question the notion that everything is unfolding according to God's plan, and that everything is developing according to the mandate hidden in some divinely ordained higher order.

Strange as it may seem, perhaps one of the most important developments in understanding the history of Christian spirituality is the effort to take history seriously, precisely *as history*. Rather than looking at history in an effort to validate present positions already held, there is an awareness that history must be looked at on its own terms, and that persons, movements, and events must be examined in historical context. We cannot simply turn our backs on history when it does not confirm what we have already decided is true. In much the same way that some use the term "traditional" to support positions of a rather recent 19th-century vintage, others look to history to find therein what they want to find. But what do we discover if we attempt to look at history on its own terms? What can we learn if we look to history honestly?

Helpful guides in this effort to take history with utmost seriousness remind us that historical context must be respected in the complex task of interpreting the history of Christian spirituality.[7] More crisply: We must accept the fact that people of earlier ages lived in situations very different from our own. And we must seek ways of allowing them to speak to our situation rather than forcing our own agenda into their lives and writings.

This throws into question the value of short, sweeping surveys of the history of spirituality, and suggests that much more care needs to be taken if we are to gain even a glimpse of how others struggled with life in Christ at earlier times and in different places. The history of Christian spirituality is less about a neat development of truths and insights over the course of time, and more about the stumbling and sometimes erratic efforts of particular individuals who tried, sometimes by fits and starts in the mess of their own history, to live in Christ by the presence of the Spirit. Spirituality in history is a story of flesh and blood people who lived lives that only later generations came to see as smooth sailing down an easy street called the spiritual life.

If history is to be viewed more honestly we need to be more critical of general chronological and narrative histories of spirituality. These histories search for historical data as background to the central task of exposing and validating received traditions. In this approach, historical factors are marshalled as evidence in support of claims already made on other bases. Thus historical scrutiny does little to alter the resounding conclusion: It has always been this way! Most views of the history of spirituality tend to lump together complex, diverse events and figures in an all too neat and tidy picture. The effect of this on contemporary Christians is a general ignorance of the rich diversity of expressions of the Christian spiritual life. It also has the effect of making us deaf to those alternative voices that have challenged and criticized the accepted, mainstream approach to Christian faith, practice, and prayer. Christian spirituality has been dominated by spiritual, cultural, and social elites. And this domination continues when we see Christian history as an inevitable, divinely ordained, progressive development.

Appropriate contemporary views of the history of Christian spirituality are shaped by the Second Vatican Council's perspective on the nature of the church and of spirituality, as well as by a guiding conviction about the importance of the experience of those who live at the margins of church and society. What is required is that we set aside our preconceptions that history is always progressing along a certain line and that things are always working out for the good. And it demands that we bracket our view of who won and who lost during a particular historical period. We are asked to resist the temptation to see in earlier periods what we want to see, thereby validating our present beliefs by our naive reading of history. Rather, we are to be attentive to the "underside of history," i.e., to take a different standpoint in order to let history have its say.[8] Viewing history from the underside also allows us to see "the other"—the losers, the poor, the outcast, those who have been pushed and shoved to the margins by the victors. Simply, it is to give those outside the mainstream a chance to be heard, recognizing that the history of spirituality is richly laden with alternative experiences.

LOOKING AGAIN

It may be instructive to look to two important features of the tradition: 1) the development of religious life, and 2) the conflict over the Beguines.[9] In the first case, religious life is commonly thought to have developed along the lines of the dominant "Pachomius to Ignatius model" made popular by David Knowles. In such a view, all expressions of religious life are an expression of the one, same impulse which was early enshrined in the monastic movement and adapted later to suit the needs of a changing church and world. This model and others like it reinforce a sense that history is simple, linear, and monolithic rather than complex and plural. From this perspective, religious life develops throughout Christian history as various expressions of an essentially unified communal, monastic way of life. In other words, different forms of religious life are variations on a theme.

But when this dominant model is set aside, and history looked at afresh, it is possible to suggest a very different scenario. The origins of religious life lie in historical settings different from and earlier than those of monastic life as we know it. Primitive Christianity witnessed the phenomenon of autonomous virgins as well as of Syriac ascetics, the *ihidaya* (single ones). It is far more likely that these two varieties of the committed single life are the two earliest instances of what is now called religious life. Thus, not only does this fresh perspective provide new insight regarding the origins and development of religious life, but it also presents a new lens for assessing contemporary expressions of religious life as they shake loose from vestiges of monastic influence and practice that are not essential to them.

In viewing the Beguines, a very popular movement of single women in the early Middle Ages, particularly in Holland and Belgium, it is ordinarily understood that their gradual disappearance should be attributed to their tendency toward unorthodox views. But if this assumption is set aside, it appears rather that the identity, indeed the very existence, of these committed lay women was effectively snuffed out because the canonical, official framework for religious life could not or would not allow for this more spontaneous, free-form expression of living the gospel. The question of whether the Beguines were orthodox or not can only be addressed properly in view of the evidence that some among them were self-taught, theologically astute, and highly sophisticated women. Consequently their theology would likely strike a note of caution among their theologically literate contemporaries: men, mostly clerics, who would have been trained in the more formal theology of the monastery or the newly emerging universities.

It is possible to appreciate the traditions of spirituality in a way that opens up fresh perspectives and future possibilities. But this requires a willingness to hear the story—and thus the voices—of those groups and persons who have been marginalized and disenfranchised not only by historical processes that are seen in terms of winners and losers, but even more by the way in which accounts of history have traditionally been passed from generation to generation.

FASHIONING A FUTURE FROM TRADITION

Approaches to history which seek out the wisdom of the tradition by means of a critical retrieval of its riches also suffer some shortcomings. What is needed in any contemporary approach to history is a strong measure of self-criticism, a willingness to constantly rework one's own assumptions and presuppositions. Many contemporary views of the history of Christian spirituality provide sharp criticism of "traditional" approaches. As has already been suggested, this critique is warranted on several counts, particularly the "traditional" emphasis on the individual, its elitism, and its lack of attention to experience as a point of entry in the spiritual life. But the tradition is rich. And so in all contemporary approaches to Christian tradition, greater attention needs to be given to the ways in which the tradition itself wages a strong critique of our present perspectives, calling into question the "presentism" which lies at the base of many of our presuppositions and guiding convictions, even as we seek to interpret history honestly.

A helpful guide in viewing the tradition with an eye to recovering its riches is Bernard McGinn. Though his concern is with the tradition of Christian mysticism in the more restricted sense, McGinn situates his discussion within the context of Christian spirituality more broadly.[10] His perspectives are helpful in many ways.

When history is taken seriously, we must put a big question mark next to many of our commonly held assumptions about the spiritual life and the mystical life. For example, the governing category for viewing the tradition of mysticism need not be solely that of union with God as is often assumed. The tradition embodies many different ways of speaking of the fullness of the spiritual and mystical life. Indeed, there is much to suggest that "presence" rather than "union" is the more appropriate category in interpreting the traditions of Christian spirituality. The spiritual traditions of Christianity, when viewed through this lens, appear quite a bit different. The spiritual life, and especially its expression in mystical experience, is not so much a matter of striving for the heights of mystical union between the soul and God who is utterly different from us. It is rather more a matter of attending to God's presence to us and responding to God's presence by being altogether present to the divine presence which is always near. Said another way, the whole of the spiritual life can be understood in terms of simple loving presence. This requires a different view of the long history of spirituality, now seen in terms of various ways of responding to God's presence and participating ever more fully in the divine life altogether present in human life, history, world, and church. Such insights call for a reevaluation of what we have thought mysticism to be, which writings we have judged central to the mystical tradition, and who we have thought the mystics to be. From the optic of "presence" rather than "union," we can glimpse the lives of many more ordinary Christians who have lived and are living in our midst a deeply mystical life in the manner of Karl Rahner's "mysticism of everyday life."[11]

If we are willing to take history seriously in our efforts to understand the history of Christian spirituality, it is possible to learn a little from it. We are able to see that the traditions of spirituality are much wider and more inclusive than we are inclined to think. There has never been one way of living an authentic spiritual life, nor one sure way to union with God. We see that the Christian spiritual tradition is like a mountain, containing within it many seams waiting to be mined. Most approaches to spirituality in history mine the same vein over and over again. What is taken from these seams is rich, indeed, but it is quite the same variety of riches brought forth again and again. Fresh perspectives on history, ones which look at history as history rather than as data to validate positions already held in the present, invite us to see that there are various seams in that same mountain, as yet untouched and equally as rich.

Sober assessments of the spiritual traditions of Christianity open up new perspectives on the past, giving every indication that there is no place in it to seek refuge. However strongly contemporary "traditional" voices exhort us to return to the tried and true ways of the past, the virtues of that old time religion, there is no going back to a golden age of the church or to a pristine spirituality of an earlier age. There never was a golden age, no virgin time of Christian spirituality. And there is no blueprint for living the Christian spiritual life in today's world.

People in every age, Francis and Clare, Mechtild, Gertrude,

Alphonsus Liguori, Jane Frances de Chantal, Cornelia Connelly, and Jean Vanier have had to seek appropriate ways to live the fullness of life in Christ by the presence and power of the Holy Spirit. There is no one way. There are many paths in the one Way who is Jesus Christ. This Spirit is at work in different cultures and different periods of time calling forth expressions of Christian life appropriate to very different ways of perceiving and being in the world. This same Spirit is at work in light of the events, hopes, sufferings, and promises of different periods of history. Francis and Dominic had very different understandings of Christ, and this gave rise to recognizably distinct spiritualities appropriate to their day and age. Ignatius of Loyola understood Christ differently still, in a way that was particularly appropriate to his time and place. The way in which Thérèse of Lisieux attempted to integrate contemplation and action is altogether different from that of the followers of Ignatius, who seek to be contemplatives in and through direct apostolic service. And this is different still from the followers of Francis of Assisi who contemplate in the brokenness of the poor, sick, and marginalized the wounds of the crucified and risen Christ. At different times and places, Christians have devised different constellations of community to allow for the charisms of its members. There are the great monastic communities throughout Christian history in which the common life is strong. Then there are the apostolic communities of women and men who band together as companions in service of the needs of the church. And then there are those who have lived as anchorites and hermits, or expressed the solitary life in some other manner, with a strong sense of offering their charism in service of the human and Christian communities.

In every age there has been the struggle to avoid mere imitation of the ways of the past, and to find new ways to take up the task of being conformed to the person of Christ and united in communion with God and with others. Sober views of history provide insight into the quite diverse ways in which people have struggled to do this.

In every age Christians should look to the tradition and to the earliest Christian communities for insight in the task of living the fullness of life in Christ in their own day, to be sure. It is the very nature of the Spirit of Christ to remind us of all that Jesus has said and done. But it is also the Spirit's work to urge us on to make a way, sometimes where there has been no way before us. And sometimes it is the work of the Spirit to give birth to expressions of Christian life which seem to have no clear precedent in the life of the church. It is precisely this that we see in the lives of the great figures of the spiritual traditions who, though they now appear traditional, gave expression to the life of the Spirit in ways that were not easily understood by the mainstream, and rarely accepted outright by those at the center of church and society.

Our understanding of the fullness of Christian life is skewed when we focus on Thomas Aquinas but not Bonaventure, Duns Scotus and many other lesser known theologians of the Middle Ages. An appreciation of Francis of Assisi and the Franciscan movement is deficient unless he is considered alongside Clare and her sisters who sought to live the gospel in the same way as the brothers did, but were restricted from doing so by ecclesiastical prohibitions. Yet it is only in recent years that the strength of Clare's legacy has been brought from the edges to occupy a more central place in the Franciscan consciousness. As this has moved from the edges to the center, fresh understandings and expressions of spirituality are emerging in the lives of the daughters and sons of Francis and Clare.

Many of those who have been pushed and shoved to the margins of Christian history are finding their way back through the efforts of those today who recognize that there is something crucial to be learned from those who have been forgotten or overlooked. In addition to the towering figures of the Christian tradition there have been those who have made their way well beyond the limelight's beam. Alongside the priests and bishops and monks and nuns who have occupied the pages of the history of Christian spirituality, there are those who have lived in the communion of sacramental marriage. Where and how are the traces of a spirituality of marital love to be gleaned from a Christian history which has exalted marriage as a sacrament but, in practice, has claimed time and again that the religious vows are a superior way of living the Christian life? And where are we to find the legacies of those who have sought God alone—alone? How does one begin to spell out a spirituality of the single life for the increasing number of people who opt to remain single today, given how little we know from and about single people "in the world" who have struggled to live the fullness of Christian life throughout history?[12] And what might be known of the spirituality of the mentally handicapped, physically disabled, cultural and racial minorities, gays and lesbians throughout Christian history if we are willing to search in unexpected places for neglected wellsprings well beyond the limelight of Christian history. The concern here is not to be "nice" or to give those who have been neglected their day in the sun. It is rooted in the conviction that something central to the task of being and becoming Christian is to be learned from those who have been hushed and hidden by the way in which the Christian story has been proclaimed and promoted.

Today we must be ever more attentive to the voices of all those who have not been heard or seen because judged unimportant to the central Christian story. Those at the margins, in the fissures, between the cracks of the tradition, demonstrate that the fullness of life in Christ by the presence and power of the Holy Spirit is not just for a religious elite.

Christian spirituality is not just one dimension of the Christian life, it *is* the Christian life. Likewise, Christian spirituality is not just for this or that spiritual or religious person in the church. It is for all the baptized who make up the Body of Christ. Seeing those at the edges of the Christian spiritual tradition striving to live the fullness of the Christian life gives reason to hope that there are many different ways to follow the Way. But, enriched by the reserves of spiritual wisdom in this tradition, ours is not to try to replicate the lifestyle or devotional practices of an earlier age. Nor is it to imitate the lives of those who have gone before us. It is rather to follow Jesus in our own day, being conformed to Christ and united in communion with God and with others. And it is to make a way, where there may seem to be no way at all, through the presence and power of the Spirit of Christ who is the Way.

CONCLUSION

In this chapter I have suggested that there is an enormous interest in the traditions of spirituality today precisely because the world in which we live seems so terribly insecure. At the risk of oversimplification, it might be said that those returning to tradition take two very different directions: First, many seek to find in it a source of refuge from the uncertainties and disorientation of our age; second, there is the attempt to retrieve the riches of the past for living in today's world with an eye to the future in which the power of love will prevail over all evil.

The widespread interest in the tradition is seen, in part, in the wide range of publications which deal in one fashion or another with the history of spirituality. The most helpful approaches to history and tradition are those which do not attempt to convey the same insights over and over again, or look at history in an attempt to validate what is already held to be true. Rather, the most helpful views of history and tradition are those which attempt to take history seriously, seeking to understand persons, movements, writings in their own context. Such approaches enable us to understand that our view of history is myopic if we insist on seeing history in terms of a neat and tidy, organic, linear development. History is quite simply more sporadic, episodic, indeed random, than that. So we must look here and there, search for clues in unlikely places, attend to details that we might be first inclined to see as insignificant, listen to voices that we might at first think are unintelligible. What we might find is that those at the edges of the tradition, those on the margins of the history which has been written by the winner about the winners and for the winners, can show us the way forward.

The future of the traditions of Christian spirituality is being shaped in great measure by the insights of the Second Vatican Council. In the next chapter we will look to key conciliar principles as central to the orienting vision guiding developments in contemporary Christian spirituality.

■ *Notes to Chapter 3* ■

1. A survey is found in Michael Downey, "Spiritual Writing, Contemporary" in *The New Dictionary of Catholic Spirituality*. Michael Downey, ed. Collegeville, MN: Liturgical Press, 1993, pp. 916–922. Perhaps the most comprehensive treatment of various figures and movements in the history of Christian spirituality in English is found in the Paulist Press multivolume series entitled Classics of Western Spirituality.

2. See John Heagle, "A New Public Piety: Reflections on Spirituality." *Church* 1 (1985), pp. 52–55.

3. Rosemary Haughton, "Prophetic Spirituality." *Spiritual Life* 35/1 (Spring 1989), p. 7.

4. Sandra M. Schneiders provides a fine exposition of the development and various usages of the term in "Theology and Spirituality: Strangers, Partners, or Rivals." *Horizons* 13/2 (1986), pp. 253–274. See especially p. 257ff.

5. See D. Catherine Brown, *Pastor and Laity in the Theology of Jean Gerson*. New York: Cambridge University Press, 1987; James L. Connolly, *Jean Gerson: Reformer and Mystic*. Dubuque: Brown, (1928) 1962.

6. Such an approach is seen in the recent work of Bradley P. Holt, *Thirsty for God: A Brief History of Christian Spirituality*. Minneapolis: Augsburg/Fortress, 1993; see also Louis Bouyer, et al., *A History of Christian Spirituality*, Vol. 1: *Spirituality of the New Testament and the Fathers*. New York: Seabury, 1963. Bouyer suggests that all Christian spirituality develops organically from the spirituality expressed in the New Testament, especially in the Johannine and Pauline writings. But he goes further to suggest that the contours of all authentic Christian spirituality are crystallized in early monasticism. For Bouyer, later developments in Christian spirituality are like variations on the one same monastic theme.

7. A good example is Philip Sheldrake, *Spirituality and History: Questions of Interpretation and Method*. New York: Crossroad, 1992.

8. The term "underside of history" has been used frequently in currents of liberation theology to describe the vantage point of those at the margins, on the edges of social, economic, and religious institutions.

9. Here I draw from the work of Philip Sheldrake, *Spirituality and History*, Part Two.

10. Bernard McGinn, *Foundations of Mysticism: Origins to the Fifth Century* (vol. 1 of *The Presence of God: A History of Western Christian Mysticism*). New York: Crossroad, 1992. This is the first volume of a projected four-volume study. The second volume has been published under the title *The Growth of Mysticism: Gregory the Great through the Twelfth Century*. New York: Crossroad, 1994. McGinn treats mysticism as a part or element of religion, as a process or way of life, and as an attempt to express a direct consciousness of the presence of God. *Foundations,* pp. xv–xvi.

11. As we have seen in the preceding chapter, "the mysticism of everyday life" is developed by Karl Rahner. See Harvey Egan's explication of this theme in his "The Mysticism of Everyday Life." *Studies in Formative Spirituality* 10/1 (1989), pp. 7–26.

12. Susan A. Muto, *Celebrating the Single Life: A Spirituality for Single People in Today's World.* 1985; reprint, New York: Crossroad, 1989.

■   *Chapter 3: For Further Reading*   ■

Louis Bouyer, et al., *A History of Christian Spirituality*. 3 vols. New York: Seabury, 1963–1969.

Christian Spirituality I, II, III (vols. 16, 17, 18 of *World Spirituality.* Ewert Cousins, gen. ed.). New York: Crossroad, 1986–1991.

Urban T. Holmes, *A History of Christian Spirituality: An Analytical Introduction*. New York: Seabury Press, 1980.

Cheslyn Jones, Geoffrey Wainwright, Edward Yarnold, eds., *The Study of Spirituality*. Oxford; New York: Oxford University Press, 1986.

Philip Sheldrake, *Spirituality and History: Questions of Interpretation and Method*. New York: Crossroad, 1992.

Richard Woods, *Christian Spirituality: God's Presence Through the Ages*. Chicago: Thomas More, 1989; rev. ed. Allen, TX: Christian Classics/ Thomas More, 1996.

Richard Woods, "Spirituality, Christian (Catholic), History of" in *The New Dictionary of Catholic Spirituality*. Michael Downey, ed. Collegeville, MN: Liturgical Press, 1993, pp. 938–946.

CHAPTER 4

Conciliar Orientations

In the first chapter attention was given to those events in recent history and those elements in contemporary culture that lie at the root of the growing interest in spirituality today. These factors need to be taken into account in considering the growth of interest in a specifically Christian spirituality. But alongside these, attention must be given to the Second Vatican Council.

Vatican Council II (1962–1965) was a gathering of primarily Roman Catholic Church leaders called together by John XXIII to look seriously at the life of the Christian in the church and in the world in light of the urgent demands and pressing needs of the people of this age. With its focus on the universal call to holiness, the importance of the Word of God in scripture, the centrality of the liturgy, and a fresh understanding of the relationship between church and world, the council gave shape to a new understanding of Christian life and practice. It could also be argued that this renaissance was already afoot and that the council was responding to changes as well as prompting them. Be that as it may, the renaissance in spirituality which followed the council extends well beyond Roman Catholicism. Many of its fundamental orientations and convictions undergird a good measure of contemporary Christian spirituality.

A HOLY PEOPLE

All who are baptized, regardless of their situation or state in life, are called to the one same holiness.[1] This is a holiness rooted in the grace of baptism. It finds its full flowering in the abundance of charity in the life of the Christian, in the believing community, and in the world. Its fruit is found in the creation of human and Christian communities more in keeping with God's intention for the world now and to come: the reign of God about which Jesus preached and for which he died.

The affirmation that all the baptized are called to the fullness of life in Christ has had significant consequences in the life of the church. People of all walks of life are now concerned with spirituality. Laypersons as well as monks, clergy, and religious enroll in courses and institutes of spirituality, engage in spiritual direction, find room in their busy lives to spend time in prayer, make annual retreats, or try to find very simple ways of discovering the contemplative dimension of everyday living. There is widespread interest in different types and styles of prayer. As a corrective to many previous approaches which emphasized the importance of celibacy and the religious vows in attaining the fullness of the Christian life, there are numerous efforts to develop approaches to Christian spirituality that give due emphasis to the varied experiences of laypeople in the church and the world.

For example, it is now more commonly recognized that many of the central features of Ignatian spirituality were developed by Ignatius Loyola before he was ordained, prior to the foundation of the Society of Jesus. The invitation to share in such a spiritual legacy, lay in its origins, is a welcome change in the current state of spirituality. It allows for a greater measure of authentic collaboration between Jesuits and laypersons, women and men, in various apostolates which, in the main, were viewed in the past as being in the hands of "the Fathers" who were aided in what was essentially their task by lay helpers. Similarly, it is useful to remember that monasticism at its roots was a lay movement. Monasticism is not an inherently clerical or canonical form of living the Christian life. Though both these expressions of spirituality, the Ignatian and the monastic, have in fact become highly clericalized, they were not so in their earliest forms. This suggests that there may be other possibilities for their expression in the future. Earlier efforts to apply the insights of both approaches to the lives of laypersons have done so through a "trickle-down" strategy. That is to say, principles were derived from Jesuit or monastic life and then applied willy-nilly to lay-people living in vastly different circumstances in the world.[2]

Recent perspectives on the particular spiritualities of religious, clergy, and monastics consciously avoid reliance on such a model of derivation, recognizing the hazards of any trickle-down spirituality.

In the postconciliar period there has been a sustained effort to cultivate a spirituality rooted in the council's universal call to holiness. There has been a focus on an authentically lay spirituality attentive to the primacy of baptismal grace, the centrality of the gospel in Christian life, and the need to recognize that holiness is both gift and task to be embraced in the midst of the ordinary and extraordinary events of everyday living. All the baptized are called to the fullness of life in the Spirit. Expressions of Christian spiritual life among the faithful cannot be understood or explained simply by extension or comparison to the paradigms of mature spirituality appropriate to clergy and religious.

Diverse spiritualities emerge as people of all walks of life face different challenges. Just a few examples will have to suffice here. There are treatments of the spiritualities which emerge in the midst of the crises and challenges of mid-life, in the course of aging, and even in the lives of those who are single by choice, circumstance, or calamity. There are spiritualities which emerge from the experience of marriage and family, as well as in the midst of separation, divorce, and remarriage. There is even a particular kind of spirituality which emerges in the experience of marriage between persons of different Christian churches. There are discussions of spirituality in view of the experience of terminal illness. These treatments of different types of spirituality are rooted in the conviction that all believers are called to the one same holiness, and that many face similar challenges and demands in the process of Christian growth and development, regardless of their lifestyle or state in life.[3]

One of the more hopeful developments on the contemporary scene concerns the understanding of religious life and priesthood. In treating the various forms of religious life there is emphasis on such a call occurring within the context of the grace given in baptism and nourished within a community of faith and sacramental worship. There is less accent on what makes the religious life different and distinct from the life of the gospel to which all are called in baptism, and more accent on the religious life as one expression of the baptismal gift and call of the whole church to be a corporate witness and sign in and to the world.[4] Likewise, helpful discussions of a spirituality of the priesthood emphasize that ordained ministry is rooted in the life of a community of grace and baptism, and is best exercised in collaboration with other ministers both ordained and nonordained, modeled on the ministry of Christ the servant.[5]

The recognition of the Spirit's presence at the heart of every form of authentic Christian life calls for the development of different approaches to prayer for people dealing with a wide range of life experiences. So, for example, Christian spirituality today focuses on the necessity of praying in the midst of all the experiences of a life, the positive ones for which we give praise and thanks to God, and the negative ones to which the appropriate response may be silence, grieving, or lament.

The flourishing of spirituality today is due to the invitation offered to each baptized Christian to take up the challenge of living the fullness of the Christian life by the presence of the Spirit. Indeed it appears that spirituality in the period since the council is, more than anything else, a lay or laical spirituality.[6] Whatever the spirituality being considered, there is the shared conviction that life in Christ by the power of the Spirit stems from membership in God's people (*laos*) who together make up the body of Christ in and to the world. Different spiritualities are expressions of this Christian mystery, and will flourish to the degree that they invite different people into fuller participation in this mystery. All this having been said, it must be recognized that ever since the council there have remained all the while signs of a defensive reaction to the reforms and renewal occasioned by the council. There is even now a strong measure of diffidence in the face of the practical implications of the universal call to holiness and to the sometimes unwieldy harvest which its cultivation might yield.

FORMED BY THE WORD

Because the council stressed the centrality of the Word in Christian faith and practice there has been much more attention to the role of sacred scripture in contemporary spirituality.[7] Just as contemporary currents in spirituality are properly understood in terms of the singular significance of the universal call to holiness, so too contemporary spirituality can only be properly understood in light of the central role which the Bible and the Word of God play in this spirituality. Indeed, contemporary spirituality is biblical spirituality. It would be impossible to summarize the number of books, articles, and essays which emphasize the Word of God as the very basis of any Christian spirituality worthy of the name. People in the church today are "hungry" for the Word of God. This is manifest in the enormous number of participants in Bible study groups, as well as in the deep desire to hear homilies that are based on the scriptures and that really address the lives of the ordinary faithful. Once thought to be in the province of Protestant Christians, scripture studies undertaken by Catholics as well as other Christians have had an inestimable influence on Christian spirituality. The desire for a scripture-based spirituality is not only expressed in the plea for more effective proclamation and hearing of the Word during the celebration of the eucharist and the broader sacramental life of the church. It also lies at the heart of the practice of daily scripture reading or meditation on the Word—no matter how short the passage or for how brief a time—that many have adopted. Said another way, the centrality of sacred scripture in contemporary spirituality is seen in the importance which the Word of God holds both in the public, liturgical life of the church as well as in the more personal or individual prayer of contemporary Christians.

To some this may not seem such an important development in contemporary spirituality. Its significance is only measured in view of preconciliar approaches to the spiritual life in which scripture played a relatively minor role. Not only were the scriptures relegated to a minor role in the Mass, but the sermon was often related only tangentially to what had been proclaimed in the epistle and the gospel. And because most of what took place during the Mass was "read" in Latin and so unintelligible to the majority in most congregations, it was far more difficult to appreciate the sacred scripture as the living Word of God. Prior to the Second Vatican Council, Catholic school children were often discouraged from reading the Bible, though they may have learned about Adam and Eve, Noah and the Ark, Naomi and Ruth, Queen Esther, or the young King David in other religious books. Instead of reading the Bible, they were encouraged to read the stories of the saints held up as models for young people: Thérèse of Lisieux, Tarcisius, Lucy, Agnes, Aloysius Gonzaga, and Dominic Savio.

By way of contrast, contemporary Christians cannot seem to get quite enough of scripture. For many it is the "acid test" for authentic spirituality. And at the base of this deep hunger for the Word of God is a desire to bring the power and presence of God's Word to bear on the task of being and becoming Christian in today's world. What does the Bible say about nuclear arms? Birth control? Abortion? Homosexuality? The ordination of women? Or ordination in general? Divorce and remarriage? The suffering of the innocent?

The great strength of this development is that the Word of God as rule of faith and gospel living is kept to the fore. All Christian spirituality is authenticated by the lordship of Christ and the power of the Spirit as discerned in the Word of God proclaimed, heard and celebrated in communion with the church. But caution is in order here. The Bible does not provide ready answers to many of the complex tasks we face in today's church and world. It is not simply a matter of finding a scriptural passage to bring to bear on a particular conundrum we face. It is a matter of looking to the Bible as the living Word of God and attending to the presence of the Spirit in the reading, proclamation, and hearing of the Word in the communion of faith and worship which is the church. It is the work of the Spirit to enable us to receive and re-receive, interpret and reinterpret, work and rework the meaning and message of the Bible in ways that allow the written word to stand forth as the Word of God living and true. Briefly, it is the task of contemporary Christians to discern the orientations, intuitions, indeed a certain *savoir-faire* communicated in the Bible so that our perceptions, motivations, and identity might be altogether transformed by the Word of God.

THE WORSHIPING COMMUNITY

Another important conciliar orientation is the attention given to the importance of liturgy, especially the eucharist, in Christian life.[8] Since in conciliar perspective the eucharist is understood as the source and summit of Christian life, the spirituality which results is shaped by this central affirmation. There is a great deal of attention given to the formative role of liturgy in the Christian spiritual life and increasing attention to the need to spell out a spirituality shaped through and through by the liturgical life of the church. Many share the conviction that liturgy is the singularly important prayer of the Christian people. Liturgy, particularly the eucharist, is the coming together of the church, the prayer in which the Christian community expresses and receives its identity as the Body of Christ. The concern shared by many in the church today may be stated simply: Christian prayer and spiritual life suffer when they are not rooted in the liturgical life of the church.

Many contemporary understandings of Christian spirituality rest on the premise that every spirituality needs to be informed by liturgy.[9] In a postconciliar perspective there seems little room for dispute on this point. Christian spirituality today is given shape by communal worship, common prayer and praise, celebration in Word and sacrament. Consequently, those who strive to live a deeply spiritual life must continually struggle with the question of just how liturgy and spirituality are related to one another. In other words: How do we make connections between what happens in church and what happens in the rest of life? How do sacraments connect with the "stuff" of real life: sexuality, political responsibility, economic accountability, child rearing, the tedium of too much work, ill health, unemployment, and so on? There is growing awareness that there is an essential connection between liturgy and life, worship and work, sacraments and spirituality. Indeed, sacramental celebration expresses an ethical horizon for Christian living.[10] In celebrating the sacraments, believers express their hope for how the world should be, and how human beings should conduct themselves in the church and in the world. In such an approach to the sacraments, the eucharist constitutes the heart and soul of a Christian ethic. In its celebration, Christians commit themselves to building a world rooted in communion and justice. Consequently, there is great attention to emphasizing the implications of the eucharist for creating a more equitable social order, drawing out the ramifications of this sacred and sacrificial meal for dealing with problems like world hunger.[11] In all of these approaches we see an articulation of the deep desire of the Christian people to take utterly seriously in their everyday living that which is said and done in liturgy.

It is an easy solution to a complex question to suggest, for example, that since the eucharist is an act of thanksgiving, Christian spirituality today must be marked by a spirit of thanksgiving. Or since the revised liturgical forms of the church give pride of place to the Word, all Christian spirituality will focus on the Word of God. There is a growing recognition that the task of integrating liturgy and life as a response to the Spirit is more complex. Christian life in the Spirit demands not only that liturgy have a formative role in Christian living, but that the spirituality of the person and community shapes liturgy. Far more than in preconciliar liturgical life, there is an awareness of mutuality of impact here. Liturgy and spirituality are to be shaped by one another. This is to say that people bring their experience to bear and they want their experience to count in the public prayer of the church. This is particularly true of many women, persons of color, the mentally and physically handicapped, and other minorities and marginalized groups in the church.[12] People bring a rich array of experiences to worship, and there is growing awareness that there must be enough room in our liturgical life to allow this rich diversity to be recognized, "named," and brought to bear on the form or expression which liturgy takes. If there is recognition that liturgy shapes spirituality and spirituality shapes liturgy, then it becomes more possible to recognize a variety of spiritualities, not just *a* or *the* liturgical spirituality, not just a *particular* liturgical spirituality. And this calls for the cultivation of a great variety of liturgical expressions, not just one. This understanding allows for dynamic interaction, openness to change under the Spirit's lead, and a multiplicity of future possibilities.

To put it in simpler terms: A great majority of people in the postconciliar church believe that liturgy, particularly the eucharist, is crucial to the Christian spiritual life. But it is a lamentable fact that relatively few have the experience of a vibrant liturgical life in which they are invited to "full, conscious, and active participation" in worship.[13] If this mandate of the council is to be carried through, then there must be a fuller recognition of the great diversity of spiritualities lived by the Christian people, and a willingness to allow the spiritualities of diverse and often marginalized persons and groups to actually change the form that liturgy takes.

One of the ways in which the diversity of spiritualities is expressed is in popular devotions, which seem to have declined somewhat in the United States in the days since the council. One question which deserves fuller attention is: What has happened to spirituality after the downplaying of popular devotions, which were the backbone of Catholic practice for so many Catholics?[14] Church leaders and theologians wanted a shift from such devotions to liturgy and sacraments, but there is ample evidence to suggest that the folks in the pews have not followed this, especially when the experience of liturgy in many places is uninspiring.

The three conciliar orientations treated thus far may be summarized quite briefly as follows: Much of the interest in spirituality today is prompted and in turn shaped by the Second Vatican Council's affirmation of the universal call to holiness, by its emphasis on the centrality of sacred scripture in Christian life and prayer, and by its vision of the liturgy, especially the eucharist, as the source and summit of Christian life. Whatever else may be said about what is happening in Christian spirituality today, it is a laical, biblical, liturgical spirituality. In the days following the council, these three elements were uniquely expressed in the Catholic charismatic renewal movement. The charismatic renewal remains an instance of a new Pentecost for millions of baptized Catholics in whom the grace of the Spirit evokes a deeper appreciation of and commitment to personal prayer, communal worship, and holiness of life formed by the Word of God. This renewal gave widespread impetus to Christian spirituality throughout the United States and beyond, and continues to do so.

In addition to these central conciliar emphases, the council's fresh vision of the relationship between church and world has resulted in significant developments in contemporary Christian spirituality. Some of these were expected; some never could have

been anticipated. What was the council's vision of the relationship between church and world?

In a word, the metaphor of the church as fortress in the face of
the evils of the world gave way to the metaphor of the church
and the world in critical dialogue. This was formulated most
clearly in the Vatican Council's "Pastoral Constitution on the
Church in the Modern World" (*Gaudium et Spes*). Such a change
in perspective was greeted with joy and hope by many in and outside the church. Certainly one of the council's most important
documents, *Gaudium et Spes* seems to be all but forgotten in
many circles today. The assumption of *GS* is that church and
world each has something to give and receive from the other.

In earlier understandings of the nature of the relationship
between church and world, prominence was given to the person of
Christ to such an extent that the importance of the Holy Spirit was
eclipsed. By and large, classical definitions of the church main-
tained that its foundation lay in the person of Jesus Christ, and in
his mission entrusted to the Twelve. In this view Christ himself
established the church and entrusted its keys to Peter. The
bestowal of the Spirit at Pentecost signalled the birth of the
church, but even more so it marked the beginning of the mission
to preach the good news to the whole world, to the ends of the
earth. Much reflection about the nature of the church was focused
on the relation between the person and work of Jesus and the
church's institutional structure. Discussions about the church's
mission to the world tended to focus on the Holy Spirit. It was an
easy move then to assert that the successors of the Twelve and
those who through ordination share in their ministry, along with
those who have an explicit ecclesiastical affiliation through public
profession of religious vows, are entrusted with the inner life of the
church, while all the others, the laity, share in the mission of the
Spirit given in baptism for the sanctification of the profane, secular realm, i.e., the mission of the church to the world.

The problem with this construal of the church-world relationship is that it rests on an unsatisfactory understanding of the

reciprocal relationship between Christ and the Spirit. It is precisely in and through the Spirit that Christ established the church as the community of disciples. When they preach, teach, heal, and live lives of mercy and compassion, they do this in the presence and by the power of the Spirit of Christ. Envisioning the church-world relationship in terms of sacred and secular, institution and charism, Christ and Holy Spirit, ministry within the church and outside the church, rests on a rupture of Christ and Spirit that finds little justification in scripture, liturgy, or sound theology. It is unfortunate that even in much contemporary discussion about ministry, some argue that the ordained and the vowed religious serve the life of the church within, whereas the mission of laity is outside the church, i.e., the world. Just as the life of Christ and Spirit is one divine life shared and poured out in human history, so there is a continuous dynamic interaction in the church-world relationship. This is appropriately expressed in the Second Vatican Council's image of the church as sacrament *in* and *to* the world.

One of the most far-reaching negative effects of focusing attention on the inner life of the church rather than on the Spirit's presence with us in human life, history, world, and church, is the neglect of social and political issues. In many earlier approaches, commitment to the spiritual life generally took the form of being charitable to those in one's immediate family and/or community and, by extension, being charitable to others in the world at large. Responsibility for the socio-political-economic order was not often thought to be an essential part of Christian spiritual life and growth. There was often a strict equation between ethics and sexual ethics. While charity was thought to be required by the call of the gospel, justice—rendering to each person according to his or her need; creating a world in which all might grow; establishing rightly-ordered relationships in accord with the providential plan of God for humanity—was regarded as desirable, but not required.

A conciliar view of church and world in critical dialogue entails the recognition that God's providential plan for the world involves absolutely every dimension of existence. Every inch and ounce of creation is embraced by the loving God in and through Jesus Christ. This demands a view of the spiritual life at once personal and relational, inclusive of every human concern and commitment, with particular attention to those who are last and least in church and world. Even and especially those who are often judged to be nonpersons, as well as all forms of nonhuman life, are unavoidably the concern of an authentic Christian spirituality attentive to all creation, human life, and indeed the whole world as the dwelling of the Holy Spirit.

The conciliar view of church and world does not allow for any subordination of the Holy Spirit to Christ, world to church, lay to ordained and religious, secular to sacred. In this perspective, the church is not the exclusive realm of Christian living. A vast array of Christian life forms emerge in response to the Spirit who enlightens, enlivens, guides, sanctifies, and heals in human life, history, world, and church. The Holy Spirit is the Spirit of God, Spirit of Christ in history and human life. There is no denying the Spirit's presence outside the church. This requires that one look for signs of the Spirit's presence in the world at large, and be open to recognize it in surprising ways and places. And it requires a willingness to respond to it in ways sometimes even more surprising.

CONCLUSION

The documents of Vatican II have provided direction for the life of the entire church. With its emphasis on the foundational and formative role of the Word, the centrality of the liturgy and especially of the eucharist, the renewed understanding of church as the people of God who are all called to one holiness, and the understanding of the church as sacrament in and to the world, the council provided the key orienting principles for a Christian spirituality at once revolutionary and firmly rooted in the richest traditions of the Christian faith. In their effort to implement these conciliar orientations, contemporary Christians have found themselves with cause for delight in the flourishing of different currents of Christian spirituality. Some are clear developments of these conciliar orientations, while others appear to have different origins and causes. To the significant currents in contemporary Christian spirituality we now turn.

■ *Notes to Chapter 4* ■

1. "Dogmatic Constitution on the Church," *Lumen Gentium*, chapter 5.

2. For an approach to monastic spirituality which seeks to avoid the hazards of the trickle-down strategy, see Joan Chittister, *Wisdom Distilled from the Daily: Living the Rule of Saint Benedict Today*. San Francisco: Harper, 1991.

3. A sampling of the different life contexts which give shape to diverse spiritualities might include Mid-life: Janice Brewi and Anne Brennan, *Mid-Life: Psychological and Spiritual Perspectives*. New York: Crossroad, 1982; Aging: Eugene C. Bianchi, *Aging as a Spiritual Journey*. New York: Crossroad, 1982; Kathleen Fischer, *Winter Grace*. New York: Paulist, 1985; Single life: Susan A. Muto, *Celebrating the Single Life: A Spirituality for Single Persons in Today's World*. 1985; reprint, New York: Crossroad, 1989; Marriage: David M. Thomas, *Christian Marriage: A Journey Together*. Wilmington, DE: Michael Glazier 1983; William P. Roberts, ed., *Commitment to Partnership: Explorations of the Theology of Marriage*. Mahwah, NJ: Paulist, 1987; Michael G. Lawler, *Marriage and Sacrament: A Theology of Christian Marriage*. Collegeville, MN: Liturgical Press, 1993; Patrick McCormick, "Divorce (and Remarriage)" in *The New Dictionary of Catholic Spirituality*. Michael Downey, ed. Collegeville, MN: Liturgical Press, 1993, p. 286; Illness: John Carmody, *Cancer and Faith*. Mystic, CT: Twenty-Third Publications, 1994.

4. See, for example, Sandra M. Schneiders, *New Wineskins: Reimagining Religious Life Today*. Mahwah, NJ: Paulist, 1986; Schneiders, *Beyond Patching*. Mahwah, NJ: Paulist, 1991; Mary Jo Leddy, *Reweaving Religious Life*. Mystic, CT: Twenty-Third Publications, 1990; Diarmuid O'Murchu, *Religious Life: A Prophetic Vision*. Notre Dame, IN: Ave Maria Press, 1991.

5. See, for example, Thomas O'Meara, *Theology of Ministry*. New York: Paulist, 1983; Edward Schillebeeckx, *The Church with a Human Face: A New and Expanded Theology of Ministry*. New York: Crossroad, 1985; Richard McBrien, *Ministry: A Theological, Pastoral Handbook*. San Francisco: Harper, 1988; Thomas Rausch, *Priesthood Today: An Appraisal*. Mahwah, NJ: Paulist, 1992; Donald Goergen, ed., *Being a Priest Today*. Collegeville, MN: Liturgical Press, 1992.

6. Some successful efforts to develop a lay spirituality include Leonard Doohan, *The Lay-Centered Church*. Minneapolis: Winston, 1984;

Elizabeth Dreyer, *Earth Crammed with Heaven*. Mahwah, NJ: Paulist, 1994; James and Evelyn Eaton Whitehead, *The Emerging Laity*. Garden City, NY: Doubleday, 1986; Edward Sellner, "Lay Spirituality" in *The New Dictionary of Catholic Spirituality*, pp. 589–596.

7. The centrality of the revealed Word is emphasized throughout the "Dogmatic Constitution on Divine Revelation," *Dei Verbum*, the conciliar document equaled in stature only by the "Dogmatic Constitution on the Church," *Lumen Gentium*.

8. See especially the Constitution on the Sacred Liturgy, *Sacrosanctum Concilium*, nos. 1 and 10.

9. For examples of this approach, see Kevin W. Irwin, *Liturgy, Prayer, and Spirituality*. New York: Paulist, 1984; Shawn Madigan, *Spirituality: Rooted in Liturgy*. Washington, DC: Pastoral Press, 1989.

10. Efforts to show the connection between sacraments and ethics include Timothy F. Sedgwick, *Sacramental Ethics: Paschal Identity and the Christian Life*. Minneapolis: Augsburg/Fortress, 1987; Michael Downey, *Clothed in Christ: The Sacraments and Christian Living*. New York: Crossroad, 1987; James L. Empereur, *The Liturgy That Does Justice: A New Approach to Liturgical Praxis*. Collegeville, MN: Liturgical Press/Michael Glazier, 1990.

11. For example, see Monika K. Hellwig, *The Eucharist and the Hunger of the World*. 2nd ed. Kansas City, MO: Sheed and Ward, 1992.

12. For example, see Marjorie Proctor-Smith, *In Her Own Rite: Constructing Feminist Liturgical Tradition*. Nashville: Abingdon, 1990; Edward Foley, ed., *Developmental Disabilities and Sacramental Access*. Collegeville, MN: Liturgical Press, 1994.

13. *Sacrosanctum Concilium*, no. 14

14. For an investigation of the importance of popular devotions in the postconciliar church, see Regis Duffy, "*Devotio Futura*: The Need for Postconciliar Devotions" in *A Promise of Presence: Studies in Honor of David N. Power*. Michael Downey and Richard Fragomeni, eds. Washington, DC: Pastoral Press, 1992, pp. 163–183.

■ *Chapter 4: For Further Reading* ■

Dennis M. Doyle, *The Church Emerging from Vatican II: A Popular Approach to Contemporary Catholicism*. Mystic, CT: Twenty-Third Publications, 1992.

Joseph F. Eagan, *Restoration and Renewal: The Church in the Third Millennium*. Kansas City, MO: Sheed and Ward, 1995.

Gerald M. Fagin, ed., *Vatican II: Open Questions and New Horizons*. Wilmington, DE: Michael Glazier, 1984.

Adrian Hastings, ed., *Modern Catholicism: Vatican II and After*. New York: Oxford University Press, 1991.

William A. Kaschmitter, *The Spirituality of Vatican II: Conciliar Texts Concerning the Spiritual Life of All Christians*. Huntington, IN: Our Sunday Visitor, 1975

Robert L. Kinast, *Vatican II: Act II–Called to Holiness*. Collegeville, MN: Liturgical Press, 1992.

Timothy G. McCarthy, *The Catholic Tradition: Before and After Vatican II, 1878–1993*. Chicago: Loyola University Press, 1994.

Timothy E. O'Connell, *Vatican II and Its Documents: An American Appraisal*. Wilmington, DE: Michael Glazier, 1986.

CHAPTER 5

Currents in Christian Spirituality

In chapter 3 we drew attention to the widespread interest in the past and in the riches of the spiritual traditions among contemporary Christians. Chapter 4 drew attention to the fundamental orientations of Vatican Council II. This chapter will look to the present scene, and attempt to describe the various currents in Christian spirituality today. Many of these currents can be traced to Vatican II for their origins. Others find their roots in different sources. Not everything in contemporary Christian spirituality is to be lauded. Discretion is necessary in the face of some of the currents in spirituality today. And so, in this chapter we shall also look at some of the problems in Christian spirituality today, and provide a key toward possible resolution.

This survey of currents in contemporary spirituality is intended to provide an update, giving indication of the shape or direction Christian spirituality will likely take as we embark on the next millennium.

Before looking to these currents in contemporary Christian spirituality, recall that spirituality does not refer to just one dimension of life, e.g., the life of the soul or the practices of prayer. In contemporary perspective, Christian spirituality is concerned with the whole of Christian life. At issue here is the fullness of life in Christ by the presence and power of the Holy Spirit, being conformed to the person of Christ and united in communion with God, others, and all creation.

Since the council there has been sustained attention to a more

90

holistic understanding of spirituality. Here "holistic" refers to the whole person, and so there is a deeper awareness of the importance of overall health in the cultivation of holiness. There is a great deal of attention to diet and exercise, a balance of work and leisure, solitude and interaction with others in the spiritual life. Rather than beginning with doctrinal formulations or theoretical explanations of Christian life, contemporary approaches to spirituality tend to begin by stressing the singular importance of the concrete experience of searching for God, and of finding appropriate ways to live out one's response to the divine initiative.

Although the meaning of the term "experience" is quite difficult to pin down, there is a strong conviction that *human experience is the very "stuff" of spirituality*.[1] "Experience" is a term used to describe whatever enters into the actual living of our lives, whether it be religious, mystical, theological, ethical, psychological, political, or physical. Thus "spiritual experience" or "religious experience" or "experience of the Spirit" does not refer solely or even primarily to esoteric phenomena or extraordinary occurrences in the relationship between God and the soul. Rather, in contemporary spirituality "experience" is a term used to speak of all that enters our lives: events, stories, relationships, commitments, sufferings, hopes, tragedies, and so on. Our lives are shaped by our response to and engagement with all of these factors as we encounter them. And so is our spirituality.

The turn to experience has been coupled with increasing attention to the specific context or *social location* within which we live out our relationships with the other, others, and God, and to the importance of the unique culture in which we live in the shaping of these relationships. Is one's experience of God primarily in and through relationship with spouse and children? In and through a commitment to missionary activity? In teaching? Or preaching? Is one's life riddled with the sufferings and tragedies brought on by economic impoverishment? Racial discrimination? Sexual abuse? Discrimination on the basis of sex or sexual orientation? Or handicap? These factors which shape one's context, one's situation in life, are to be considered if experience is to be taken as the point of entry in the spiritual life. All of this reflects a deepening appreciation for the particular, the specific, and for differences which at times appear so great as to be irreconcilable.

Without doubt one of the most important currents in spirituality today is the awareness of alterity or *alternative experience* in the Christian spiritual life.[2] There is no one way to pray, and no single path of growth and development in the Spirit. This is a perennial truth, recognized in every age. But, perhaps as never before, there is appreciation for diversity of experiences and a commitment to search for experiences in traditions that have been overlooked and forgotten. And so there is consideration of the spiritual lives of children, of African Americans, of Hispanic Americans, of the mentally and physically handicapped, of peoples of the Third World, of gays and lesbians. In attending to the alternative experiences of those persons and groups who have not been given much room in our mainstream understanding of Christian life and spirituality, there is an emergent shared conviction that these experiences count, they matter, and that without them our understanding of Christian life in the Spirit is impoverished because of our neglect of them. This impoverishment of Spirit is true not only of the persons and groups whose experience is viewed as alternative or marginal to those in the mainstream. It is also true of those in the mainstream who tend to overlook or block out the witness and the voices of those who are pushed and shoved to the margins of church and society. For example, increasing numbers of people have found that in looking to the lives and hearing the voices of those who are handicapped, they learn not only about the alternative experience of the handicapped, but also about what it means to be human.[3] The qualities of heart such as compassion, celebration, forgiveness, and care that emerge in the encounter with these persons are indispensable for the full flourishing of life in Christ. But these qualities are sometimes unavailable to the healthy, strong, intelligent, and robust except in the encounter with "the other" of the handicapped or marginalized. Much the same could be said regarding all those persons and groups at the edges of church and society. The experience of such persons, and of the countless women who have often been invisible and powerless in church and society, has become an increasingly important, indeed indispensable, source for reflection on the nature of authentic Christian life and practice.

Undoubtedly the most important reserve of alternative experience in Christian spirituality today is *women's experience* in the church.[4] It may seem odd to refer to women's experience as alternative or marginalized since women constitute the numerical majority of Roman Catholics. But women have often been voiceless and invisible in decision-making and in the exercises of power and authority that shape their lives. In terms of the history of Christian spirituality, there are, of course, the towering figures of Teresa of Avila and Catherine of Siena, Doctors of the Church, as well as a host of others. By and large, however, women have given shape to a tradition which has remained hidden in the life of the church. Approaches to the spiritual life of women in Christian history have tended to emphasize the cultivation of the dispositions of humble service, patience, forbearance, and other virtues of the hidden life at Nazareth as exemplified in Mary, Virgin and Mother. On the other hand, courage, zeal, fortitude and other more public or social virtues have been cultivated in men. Sober readings of history are yielding a different view of women such as Hadewijch of Brabant, Hildegard of Bingen, Mechtild of Magdeburg, Julian of Norwich, Jane Frances de Chantal, Cornelia Connelly and many others who, until recently, have often occupied space only in the footnotes of the history of Christian spirituality. The recovery and retrieval of the hidden strengths of women's experience in the Christian spiritual tradition is just one factor in a much wider effort of women in today's church to recognize the importance of their own unique experience in the task of growth and development in the spiritual life.

In Roman Catholic circles, many women have sought to explicitly incorporate liberationist and feminist perspectives in their reflection.[5] Though there is a strong current of resistance to such positions in an attempt to provide rationale and spiritual resources for more traditional gender roles, far more significant for Christian spirituality today and for its future are the efforts of those who are creating possibilities for the full participation of women in every sphere of the church's life. The efforts of Christian feminists contribute to the growing awareness that women's own experience, neglected and ignored by men and women in the past and in the present, is a privileged locus for encountering the presence and action of the Spirit. Feminist Catholics, both women and men, share the conviction that the Christian tradition has been diminished by patriarchal bias and male domination in the church. The fullness of the experience of God in Christ through the Spirit is muted when women's experience is seen as alternative, written off in marginal notation, suppressed or brushed to the edges of Christian consciousness.

As never before, the experience of women as women is now being brought to bear upon understandings of God, Christ, Spirit, church, sacraments, ministry, power, and the very nature of the Christian spiritual life. At the risk of gross oversimplification, women are just now beginning to speak in their own voice, many finding in the conversation that women's ways of knowing and experience are quite different from men's.[6] Some, however, question the very assumption that women's experience differs, in principle, from men's. Others still, particularly women of color, give voice to yet other perspectives such as the womanist (African-American) and *mujerista* (Hispanic/Latina), challenging feminist theologians to look more deeply into the diversity of experience among women from different races and classes.

In identifying the currents in contemporary spirituality it is important here to note the emergence of a men's movement, proponents of which attempt to articulate features of a masculine spirituality in contrast to a feminist spirituality.[7] The premise undergirding the men's movement is that the experience of men precisely as men is not to be denigrated or suppressed in the effort to redress the wrongs inflicted on women in a church and society deeply rooted in patriarchal bias and male domination. Whether this more recent movement is complementary to a Christian feminist spirituality or in opposition to it is a subject of ongoing debate. Whatever the outcome of the debate it is altogether clear that the recognition of the importance of women's experience and the emergence of feminist spiritualities is one of the most significant, albeit unanticipated, developments in the church since the Second Vatican Council.

One of the features of contemporary spirituality which has emerged precisely as women speak in their own voice about their own experience is the singular importance of the *relational matrix* of all life. The question of whether women's ways of experiencing and knowing is different from men's gives rise to the issue of whether relationships are indeed more central to women's consciousness and experience than men's. Whatever the answer to this complex question, women's perspectives have consistently served as a reminder of the relational matrix of all human life and Christian life, and therefore of the singular importance of relationship as a governing category of the Christian spiritual life.

The attention given to the relational matrix is not limited to interpersonal relationships with others and God. It pertains to the essential relatedness of everything that exists. Such a perspective helps to undercut dualism of all sorts. With the relational matrix to the fore, there is a recognition of the importance of distinguishing rather than unduly separating soul and body, spirit and flesh, church and world, sacred and profane—all of which are ineluctably related to one another. By setting aside subtle and not so subtle dualist convictions, it is possible for contemporary Christians to embrace a more incarnational and sacramental approach to spirituality. Perhaps nowhere is the affirmation of the relational matrix of the spiritual life more conspicuous than in the attention given to interpersonal relationships, inclusive of intimacy and sexuality, with particular attention to the sacredness of marriage as the paradigmatic human relationship which discloses the divine.

In the vocabulary of spirituality today, then, it is important to note that relationality and relationship are key. This is not primarily because of the experience of women who, in the view of many, are usually more deeply sensitive than men to relationality as a governing category of life and spirituality. The conviction about the centrality of relationship in the spiritual life is rooted in the uniquely Christian understanding of God. Since the God of the Christian people, the Trinity, is a communion of persons in loving relationship, it is important to see human relationality as a privileged locus for the encounter with God.[8] Because the uniquely Christian way of speaking of God affirms that God is a communion of divine and human persons in loving relationship, it is our capacity for relationship which is the very image of God in us. Relationality is the matrix wherein we are to be conformed to the person of Christ by the presence and power of the Spirit.

But human relationships have an inherently dark side, a seemingly unavoidable negative dimension. And this demands that we seek constantly to establish rightly ordered relationships more in accord with the life of Jesus and the reign of God about which he preached and for which he died. Rightly ordered relationships are those built on mutuality, reciprocity, equality, care, compassion, justice, all with particular attention to the needs of the wounded and the weak, the last and the least. To this end, there is great interest in finding ways to take the relational matrix as it bears on the interpersonal nature of Christian life with utmost seriousness.

In addition to the emphasis on the interpersonal, there is also a growing recognition of the implications of our relationships for the creation of a new social order built on dignity of persons, mutuality, reciprocity, equality. Thus there has been considerable attention to the practical implications of Christian faith and spirituality for the transformation of social arrangements and the political order. Without doubt, this interest in social justice is one of the most significant developments in contemporary spirituality.

Such an accent underscores the importance of the practical implications of Christian life and spirituality, not just in the realm of one's interpersonal relationships with others and God, but in absolutely every sphere of life. In contemporary spirituality there is considerable attention to *praxis*. In shorthand, the term "praxis" means practice. But in contemporary theology and spirituality praxis does not describe merely any action or practice, but the practice of the gospel through which persons and communities do the truth in love freely, and in so doing enable others to do the truth in love freely, thereby participating more fully in the mystery of Christ who is contemplated in Christian prayer.

Previous approaches to the spiritual life affirmed that charity was a requirement in the pursuit of perfection, whereas justice was desirable. There would be little room for disagreement today, however, that the *creation of a just social order* is an unmistakable fruit of the life lived in Christ's Spirit. Justice is required, not simply desired. Christians at all points of the continuum, from the most conservative and traditional to the most progressive on the far left, would agree that any authentic spirituality has consequences for life in society. What these consequences might be, and how the causes of social problems are to be remedied is an area in which there will remain a great measure of disagreement for years to come. But the engagement with social concerns on the part of persons such as Mother Teresa of Calcutta, Jean Vanier, and Dorothy Day elicits strong praise by both conservative and liberal groups and publications.

Though many more conservative persons and groups would be hesitant to recognize the influence of liberation theology on their work with the poor and disenfranchised, the contours of most socially oriented spiritualities are shaped by the central role given to liberating praxis in political and liberation theologies.[9] Many of these orientations toward a spirituality of social justice were enhanced by the example of the Society of Jesus, which at its 32nd General Congregation (December 2, 1974–March 7, 1975), reexpressed the mission of the Jesuits in the postconciliar church as "the service of faith and the promotion of justice."[10] This insight into the inseparability of faith and justice has often been expressed by Jesuits and others as "the faith that does justice." Such an orientation has resulted in countless Jesuits, as well as members of other religious congregations, joining in the struggle for human dignity which forms the crux of the many different contemporary expressions of spirituality grounded in an engagement with the promotion of social justice. And the recognition of the demands of justice in the Christian spiritual life has drawn even greater attention to the issue of women in church and society, and to the struggle to work for the equality of women in all spheres of life.

The development of a stronger *ecological consciousness* may be seen as a further expression of the awareness of the relational matrix of all human and Christian life.[11] From this perspective, the environmental crisis we now face has been brought on, in part, by ignorance and misunderstanding, indeed by an irresponsible exercise of power on the part of human beings in their relationship to nonhuman life and to the goods of the earth. Some approaches to the ecological crisis are rooted in a purely pragmatic concern: we have used up the planet's resources, have raped the goodness and purity of the earth. Life as we know it cannot continue if we continue on the same course. Some draw attention to the holiness, indeed the sacredness, of creation, as well as the formative role of environment and geography in the shaping of particular spiritualities. Creation is God's gift and is not to be misused or destroyed. The whole creation is enlivened by the Spirit of God, manifests the image of God, participates in the very life of God. But, again, this is true not only of human beings, but of the whole created order. Catherine LaCugna's trinitarian perspective on creation is most instructive here:

> God is so thoroughly involved in every last detail of creation that if we could truly grasp this it would altogether change how we approach each moment of our lives. For everything that exists—insect, agate, galaxy—manifests the mystery of the living God.[12]

In this view, Jesus' offer of salvation is not just for the human race, but for the whole world. The redemptive mystery is inclusive of every inch and ounce of creation.

In emphasizing the relational as disclosive of the holy, great attention has been given to the importance of *community* in contemporary spirituality. This is seen in the great deal of attention given to the role of the assembly in the liturgical life of the Christian people, as well as in the emphasis on the parish and parish renewal, and to the local church community. But in terms of Christian spirituality, the most significant expressions of community are the emerging small faith communities. These include those ranging from parish renewal groups, prayer-study groups, Marriage Encounter, Cursillo, and the innumerable prayer groups of the charismatic renewal. In Central and South America there has been the emergence of *communidades de base*, small communities of Christians who gather together to pray, to meditate on the Word of God, and to seek ways to put the liberating message of the gospel into practice in a way that really advances the cause of justice and freedom of persons and communities. In this sense these small communities have sprung up for the purpose of self- and mutual-help. These groups, which see themselves as the basic cells of the church, have had enormous impact on the church in the Third World, especially in Latin America, and are now thriving in the churches of Africa and Asia. They have provided inspiration for spiritual renewal all over the world.[13]

It may seem that such a strong emphasis on the relational and on community as the very context of spiritual growth and development might muddle the singularly important role of human freedom, respect for individual difference, and personal uniqueness. In other words, in such a climate of relationality and community, has individual and personal responsibility for growth, transformation, Christian holiness been eclipsed? And what about some measure of solitude, a feature which has always been affirmed as indispensable for maturation in the spiritual life? Though there is some cause for concern here, the temptation is almost always to err in the other direction, as we have seen in the "traditional" approaches to spirituality with their recurrent stress on the individual often at the expense of clear communal sensibility.

The attention to individuation, the lifelong process of coming to be the persons we are called to be, precisely in and through our relationships with others and God, is particularly apparent in a current in contemporary spirituality which, though certainly not novel in the history of Christian spirituality, has been given unique emphasis in our own day. This is the perennial search for the authentic, *true self* from beneath layers of falsehood, pretense, and deceit. Perhaps the figure who has epitomized this journey of discovery of the true self from beneath layers of the false self, the illusory self, is Thomas Merton.[14] For Merton, the true self is not the self we try so hard to construct in the face of the subtle and overt pressures and expectations of others. It is a self that is already given, a vulnerable and hidden mystery deep within the heart of the person. It is the Christ who lies within each one. Although the true self is already given at the heart of each one, it is no small task to uncover it and to live in accord with it.

Since Merton's untimely death in 1968, many others have recognized the importance of this quest, particularly in light of those social, cultural, economic, and religious forces which dehumanize and hinder authentic human identity, development, and freedom. In contrast to earlier approaches to the deepest mystery of personal identity, contemporary understandings reflect a reliance on insights and wisdom from a wide range of sources, drawing from biblical sources, psychology (especially developmental psychology), theology, history, and pastoral experience.

Many search beyond a particular religious tradition, in keeping with the ecumenical and interreligious sensibility characteristic of religious and theological insight since the Second Vatican Council. Thomas Merton's quest for the true self led him to search beyond the traditions of Roman Catholicism and Christianity, even so far as to recognize the truth when he found it in the religions of the Far East. His own religious or mystical experience at Polonnaruwa in Sri Lanka is considered by many to be a very important moment, a crucial point in the long journey toward the discovery of his true self in God which is at the same time a self related to God, others, and the whole creation.

In many developments in Christian spirituality today there is a strong conviction that human development and spiritual development are interrelated. Consequently, there is a close *connection between psychology and spirituality* in contemporary spirituality.[15] There may be reason to be concerned that the distinction between the two may not be drawn sharply enough. For example, there is often a lack of clarity about the difference between spiritual direction, pastoral counseling, and psychotherapy.[16] Anyone who has been engaged in spiritual direction, counseling, or therapy will be aware that the matter appropriate to one often creeps into the other. It is far too facile a solution to suggest that spiritual direction deals with the matter of one's relationship with God, whereas counseling and psychotherapy focus on "life issues" or problems with self-identity or personal relationships. Our relationship with God ineluctably involves others and, for the person of faith, human self-identity and relationships with others always bear upon our relationship with God.

Of the many types or schools of psychology, two have been particularly influential in contemporary spirituality. The first of these might be referred to loosely as developmental psychology. From this perspective, a person moves through various stages or steps, growing and changing throughout the course of a lifetime. Drawing upon the investigations of Robert Kegan and of Carol Gilligan, the theory of cognitional development articulated by Jean Piaget, of moral development spelled out by Lawrence Kohlberg, and of faith development delineated by James Fowler, Joann Wolski Conn has attempted to apply their insights to issues of spiritual development.[17] In this view, there are recognizable sorts of spiritual experiences appropriate to persons at different developmental stages. And by recognizing normal developmental patterns, it is easier to identify aberrations and so suggest strategies to remedy them. It becomes somewhat easier to detect what is inappropriate and in need of fuller development in the task of spiritual maturation. By identifying the experiences and behaviors characteristic of fuller development, persons can be encouraged to move forward with a sense of what might be anticipated as one grows in the life of the Spirit.

Insights on these theories, and related developments in self-psychology and object relations theories and their contribution to Christian spirituality have been found most helpful, as are the efforts of those who try to bring contemporary psychological investigations to bear on the Christian contemplative and mystical traditions.

A second highly influential current in this regard is the enormous popularity of personality type indicators.[18] Perhaps the most popular of these is the Myers-Briggs personality type indicator. Based on the investigations of Carl Jung, the Myers-Briggs is designed to enable people to understand their own strengths and weaknesses, to accept and cultivate strengths and gradually correct weaknesses. Briefly, it is an instrument for self-understanding so that one comes to a deeper awareness of the givenness of one's personality: Am I an extrovert or an introvert? Do I make decisions on the basis of feelings or rational principles? Are you inclined to make a decision promptly or are you willing to let things run their course? At the risk of oversimplification, these are some of the questions which the Myers-Briggs type indicator attempts to answer, with the hope of bringing one to a fuller degree of self-knowledge and acceptance. It is useful to note that this type indicator is not only used by individuals but also by small groups and communities, even by corporations, to arrive at a better understanding of the individuals involved so as to draw on the strengths and compensate for the weaknesses or shortcomings of each.

In some currents of Christian spirituality there is reliance on the Enneagram, a type of spiritual technology or system for self-understanding and personal transformation. The Enneagram has enjoyed enormous popularity.

Perhaps the attraction to such personality type indicators is rooted in the conviction that self-awareness and self-understanding are essential in the process of spiritual growth and development. The deeper my understanding of my own strengths and weaknesses, the more I am able to respond to the healing and sanctifying grace that brings about personal transformation. Similarly, the more I understand my own temperament, the more I can seek and find suitable ways of prayer to which I am better suited as well as spiritual disciplines which might serve as a corrective and a challenge. In other words, through better self-knowledge, I am able to recognize the particular path of maturation, indeed holiness, to which I am summoned over the course of a lifetime.

One of the more helpful developments in this area is the attention given to the cultivation of different prayer forms based on an appreciation of personality types. The fundamental insight here seems to be that different psychological types are inclined to different ways of experiencing the world, God, and others. For example, introverts and extroverts live and relate to the world quite differently, as do perfectionists and those who tend to be more "laid back." And those of a more melancholic disposition have a different task of personal and spiritual integration than do those who are inclined to excitement and enthusiasm. It is important to keep in mind that such personality indicators are descriptive rather then evaluative. It is not better to be an extrovert rather then an introvert. But realizing and accepting what one is can liberate one from self- or socially imposed expectations. Again, the insight here is that such different ways of experiencing the world call for different approaches or styles of praying if one is to grow and develop in the Spirit.

The openness to various psychological insights and to other sources of insight into the dynamics of personal and spiritual growth is indicative of the conviction that approaches to Christian spirituality must be *interdisciplinary*. Closely related to this is the conviction that Christian spirituality must be informed by *ecumenical/interreligious* sensibilities. This is seen in the increasing numbers of devout Christians who have developed Zen and yoga techniques as part of their spiritual discipline. It is evident, further, in the openness of many to pray with and learn from those in other Christian churches.

In many currents of spirituality there is a recognition of the need to make connections between prayer and prophetic service, that there exists a *reciprocal relationship between prayer and action*. The authentic self known in self-scrutiny and in prayer, as well as in and through relationship with others and the whole of creation, is the self which is given by nature and developed in a lifelong process through grace and Spirit. Such development requires commitment to ongoing self-scrutiny and willingness to risk and change. But this self-scrutiny extends beyond the province of the individual to include a mature critical consciousness vis-à-vis the social-symbolic order with its dominant and often oppressive ideology. Without such critical consciousness there is a tendency to overlook the truth that any authentic Christian spirituality is intrinsically relational, social and, indeed, political. That is to say that it pertains to every dimension of our lives as persons and as a people. Spirituality does not solely concern "me and Jesus." Nor is its exclusive focus the domain of personal salvation or sanctification. Spirituality describes a way of living in Christ: being conformed to the person of Christ and being united in communion with others, the whole of creation, and with God.

Just as most developments in spirituality accept that human and spiritual development are interrelated and complementary processes, so too is there a deep conviction that prayer and action are two dimensions of the human person that are to be held together in a noble tension and an ever-deepening integration. This must be understood against the background of a long tradition that tended to separate, even set in opposition, the active life and the contemplative life. Of course, the contemplative life was judged as superior to the active life. Without prejudice to the complexity of the issue, it may be said that there is a deeper recognition today that prayer and action are rooted in one same source, the human person, who is called to the prayer of loving attention, gratitude, and praise for the presence and action of God in human life, history, world, and church, and to the activities whereby God's reign is advanced, especially through the works of prophetic service and the promotion of peace and justice.

There is a noticeable *multiplicity of spiritualities* on the contemporary scene. These emerge from the diverse experiences of the Spirit in today's church and world. And such diversity is a great richness. But, at times, it appears that there are whole industries which have developed for the promotion of particular spiritualities: the charismatic movement, Focolare, RCIA, spirituality for mid-life, Thomas Merton, centering prayer, meditation in the mode of John Main. To this must be added a word about the phenomenon of professionalization in Christian spirituality. As but two examples of this tendency, there is now a professional organization of spiritual directors throughout the world, Spiritual Directors International, as well as an international organization of retreat directors and members of retreat house teams, Retreats International. Such a tendency toward professionalization in spirituality today may be required as those who seek to live in Christ struggle with new and complex demands at the end of the 20th century. But there is always the risk that some will attempt to harness the freedom and spontaneity of the Spirit because of a concern for the canons of professionalization.[19] The resolution, of course, lies in the balance between respect for professional standards and openness to the spontaneous Spirit.

Finally, more, but still insufficient attention is being given to the impact of *science and technology* upon spirituality. This is an issue that awaits more mature and rigorous investigation in the future.

PROBLEMS

It has already been noted that the Christian spiritual traditions have both strengths and weaknesses. The survey of currents in contemporary spirituality has drawn attention to its strengths, which are all the more apparent in view of the weaknesses of earlier approaches. But there are problems as well in some contemporary approaches to spirituality, and it is to these that consideration must be given. These problems are symptomatic of the culture in which we live, and so they affect the state of spirituality in general. But they take on a particular cast against the horizon of a specifically Christian spirituality.

As might be expected, some odd ideas have accompanied changes in currents and perspectives in Christian spirituality. On one hand there is the tendency to let experience free-float. On the other hand, there is the effort to categorize rich and diverse spiritual experience far too neatly by reliance on tools like the Myers-Briggs personality type indicator or the Enneagram. In either case, serious reflection and discernment are avoided. Such tendencies bespeak deeper problems that present tough sticking points in the area of Christian spirituality today.

Even though contemporary currents and perspectives emphasize more holistic and integrative approaches to the Christian life, the common perception is still that spirituality is primarily concerned with the life of the soul, the interior life, one's prayer life, one's spiritual life, as a separate component of the Christian life. The tendency to equate the spiritual life with the interior life is particularly prevalent in our own day. Traditions that once provided a cohesive worldview and sense of belonging no longer do so for a growing number of people. Worship, Bible, and tradition no longer offer the sense of unity, clarity, and security which they once did. And so there is a flight inward, into deeper and deeper levels of the self as outer worlds of meaning seem increasingly unreliable and on the brink of collapse. Personal identity once shaped by the shared customs and traditions of neighborhood, community, or parish, is now sought in spirituality by those disaffected by or indifferent to religion. Such a tendency is found in the pious and devout who take flight to Medjugorje or enroll in the Blue Army, as well as in those post Christians who live by the light of a New Age. In both cases, spirituality is focused on the interior world of feelings and imagination with little if any explicit attempt at integrating the humdrum, the tedium of too much work, the demands of socio-political responsibility, or economic accountability.

An even more persistent problem in some approaches to Christian spirituality today is its often near-narcissistic self-preoccupation. The lingo of "my spiritual life," "my prayer life" is indicative of this. Whether one finds the culprit in the climate of the post-Enlightenment view of the human subject, or in the individualistic habits of North Americans, it is helpful to recognize that Christian spirituality has been afflicted with a brand of individual self-focus with longer and deeper roots.

It may seem unbecoming to apply any criticism whatsoever to Augustine, a figure so imposing by his insight, erudition, and balance. Augustine's theology has had a deep and lasting influence on the history of Western Christian spirituality. Whether Augustine intended it or not, his version of contemplation and ascent to God through descent into the self muted the relational and communitarian dimensions of the Christian life. His theological reflection on the Trinity was focused on the structure of God's intradivine life, that is, the relationships of Father, Son, and Holy Spirit to one another. Augustine favored images of the Trinity drawn from the psychology of the human person, understood to have the faculties of intellect, will, and memory. He believed that the structure of the individual human soul was a mirror image of the Trinity. By knowing oneself, one would know God.

Much contemporary reflection of Christian spiritual life is rooted in an approach to the Trinity emphasizing the intradivine life, mirrored in the inner life of the individual person. Knowing God means knowing the self in itself, in an ever deeper journey inward. There is always the danger that an unchecked pursuit of a personal spirituality will amount to nothing more than a narcissistic self-absorption and self-preoccupation. Augustine was certainly correct that the human person is a unique locus of the divine self-disclosure. And, given that we are created in the image and likeness of God, it is natural to look for the contours of that image within ourselves. However, Genesis 2–3 suggests that the image of God is to be found in the relationship between female and male, which gives the divine image in us a dimension beyond the solitary self.

In recent years, it appears that the therapeutic has emerged as the primary framework for understanding the spiritual life, so much so that it seems to have eclipsed the salvific as the governing category in spirituality. The typology of Myers-Briggs and the Enneagram has become virtually synonymous with spirituality in some circles. The result is that spirituality has become jargon-ridden. The language about Christ and Christ's mysteries has receded into the background as voices exhorting us about "getting in touch with anger" and the need for "quality time" and the importance of "taking care of me" hold center stage.

Without doubt one of the more hopeful developments in contemporary spirituality is the affirmation of the complementarity of human and spiritual development. The insights of psychological investigations, especially the contributions of developmental psychology, have been most helpful in understanding the dynamic of human and Christian life. But it remains true that Christianity is more than psychology. The hope which motivates the Christian is not sustained by deeper and deeper penetration of the unconscious, getting to the root of one's "life issue." Rather, it is buoyed up by looking to a promise of a future restoration, even and especially of one's own woundedness and weakness, fragility and brokenness, in and through the grace of Christ.

Perhaps underlying some of these problems in Christian spirituality is a view of God as useful. Friends, colleagues, and parishioners report unabashedly that their day just doesn't seem to go right if they don't take time for daily prayer. God seems to be an instrument, and prayer an exquisitely fashioned tool in service of a higher goal, that is, the cultivation of one's spiritual life. Even in those approaches to spirituality that do not dabble in self-focus and self-fix—for example, those with a strong and clear social justice orientation—there can be tightly held convictions about God as a means of bringing about a particular sort of social program. In the face of such a distortion, authentic Christian spirituality challenges us to believe in God simply because God is God.

There is a sense in which there is only one Christian spirituality, rooted in the Trinity and lived in light of the Incarnation and the coming of the Spirit. At the same time, the history of Christian spirituality is a story of a great diversity of approaches to the Christian life, different schools or types of spirituality, e.g., Franciscan, Ignatian, apophatic, the French school, and so on. Today there is an awareness of a plethora of spiritualities, the way in which each unique person embodies the Christian message, or, in the African-American tradition, "how your God does you." There is a great flourishing of diverse spiritualities. There is a spirituality of the mid-life crisis, of aging, of separation and divorce. There is a spirituality of the single and of the vowed.

There is spirituality for ministry and the priesthood. Then there is African-American spirituality, Hispanic-American spirituality, feminist spirituality, and male spirituality. There are those who insist quite passionately on spelling out the contours of a distinctively liturgical spirituality.

Cultural differences, diversity of social location, and vastly different situations in life require attention to the manifold ways in which the Holy Spirit is at work in persons within a culture, in relation to different traditions, and in light of the urgent demands and exigencies of different ages. But it is not altogether clear that this proliferation of spiritualities has not overshadowed elements of a common approach to the spiritual life in which all participate by virtue of baptism, regardless of the distinctiveness of their walk of life. Put more crisply, particular spiritualities must not obfuscate the ground in which all are rooted and which binds them. And this, of course, is the primacy of charity.

THE CROSS AS CORRECTIVE

In light of the problems which plague Christian spirituality today, is there some possible resolution? From the perspective of a specifically Christian spirituality, the cross is the vital center for reflection and discernment, and provides a check against the pitfalls noted above. All Christian spirituality has the paschal mystery—the passion, death, and resurrection of Christ—as its touchstone and norm. One of the more pressing challenges facing those who seek to develop a deep spirituality is to avoid the tendency to let spiritual experience free-float, untethered from its roots in Christian life and teaching. This calls for the integration of a wide range of spiritual experiences into the redemptive mystery of Christ's dying and rising to new life. But an equally important challenge is to find ways of discerning and describing those expressions of authentic Christian spiritual experience which do not fit into inherited categories for understanding and speaking of Christ's cross and of redemption in him. Above all, it is the task of all who live in Christ to continually look for the most compelling signs of the redemptive mystery in those manifestations of the Spirit which seem to be without precedent in the life of the church.

One of the most significant achievements in recent approaches to Christian spirituality is the recovery of forgotten traditions, of spiritual experience gone unnoticed. Contemporary approaches stress the importance of attending to alternative experience, of looking to the lives of those who have been pushed to the periphery of church and society, of seeking the self-disclosure of God in marginalized persons and groups as well as marginalized dimensions of the self. The task before those who seek to live an authentic Christian spirituality today is to find ways of describing and integrating a vast array of such experience in light of the mystery of the cross. Of course such a retrieval presents enormous difficulties to some currents of spirituality. The strongly patriarchal view of God and God's salvation in and through the cross of Christ, characteristic of many approaches to spirituality, puts a heavy burden on Christian feminists. The way in which the cross was and is the emblem of crusaders of different types and periods presents a whole range of obstacles not easily hurdled. But oppressive symbols of salvation are now giving way to images of the black Nazarene of non-Western, non-white cultures, and of the despised and rejected Compassion of God living in solidarity with the wounded and the weak, the last and the least, unto death and into hell.

Christian spirituality today is not a free and easy ride. Careful discernment and reflection are required in our efforts to live the fullness of life in Christ.

CONCLUSION

This chapter has drawn attention to several notable currents in Christian spirituality today. Some of these find their roots in the orientation given to contemporary Christian spirituality by the Second Vatican Council. Others have their impetus in other sources. Drawing attention to these various developments is not intended to imply that any and all authentic Christian spirituality must include each of these dimensions. It is meant to suggest, however, that Christians need to be ever more attentive to the manifold and often surprising ways in which the Spirit is at work in the church and in the world. And because some of these currents in spirituality today have brought with them chaff as well as wheat, wise discernment and sober judgment are required, as always. Helpful in that task is the discipline of studying spirituality. It is to the various ways of approaching the study of Christian spirituality that we turn in the next chapter.

■ *Notes to Chapter 5* ■

1. See Kenneth Leech, *Experiencing God: Theology as Spirituality*. San Francisco: Harper and Row, 1985. Tad Dunne, "Experience" in *The New Dictionary of Catholic Spirituality*. Michael Downey, ed. Collegeville, MN: Liturgical Press, 1993, pp. 365–377.

2. For examples of alternative experiences of Christian life, see Leonardo Boff, *Faith on the Edge: Religion and Marginalized Existence*. 2nd ed. Robert Barr, trans. Maryknoll, NY: Orbis Books, 1991. See also Brett Webb-Mitchell, *Unexpected Guests at God's Banquet: Welcoming People with Disabilities into the Church*. New York: Crossroad, 1994.

3. I have attempted to demonstrate how "normal" people can learn something crucial about Christian life from the alternative experience of the mentally handicapped in *A Blessed Weakness: The Spirit of Jean Vanier and l'Arche*. San Francisco: Harper & Row, 1986.

4. See Rosemary Radford Ruether, *Sexism and God-Talk: Toward a Feminist Theology*. Boston: Beacon, 1983; Elisabeth Schüssler Fiorenza, *In Memory of Her: A Feminist Theological Reconstruction of Christian Origins*. New York: Crossroad, 1983; Anne E. Carr, *Transforming Grace: Christian Tradition and Women's Experience*. San Francisco: Harper & Row, 1988; Elizabeth A. Johnson, *She Who Is: The Mystery of God in Feminist Theological Discourse*. New York: Crossroad, 1992.

5. For a treatment of the major themes in theology from feminist perspective, see Catherine Mowry LaCugna, ed., *Freeing Theology: The Essentials of Theology in Feminist Perspective*. San Francisco: Harper, 1993.

6. Perhaps the best known articulation of this position is Carol Gilligan, *In a Different Voice*. Cambridge, MA: Harvard University Press, 1982.

7. See Patrick Arnold, *Wildmen, Warriors and Kings: Masculine Spirituality and the Bible*. New York: Crossroad, 1992.

8. See Catherine Mowry LaCugna, *God for Us: The Trinity and Christian Life*. San Francisco: Harper, 1991, especially Part Two.

9. See Segundo Galilea, *The Way of Living Faith: A Spirituality of Liberation*. San Francisco: Harper & Row, 1988; Gustavo Gutiérrez, *We Drink from Our Own Wells: The Spiritual Journey of a People*. Maryknoll, NY: Orbis, 1984.

10. General Congregation 32, Decree 4: "Our Mission Today: The Service of Faith and the Promotion of Justice." See *Documents of the 31st and 32nd General Congregations of the Society of Jesus*. St. Louis, MO: Institute of Jesuit Sources, 1977. See also Pedro Arrupe, *Justice with Faith Today*. Jerome Aixala, ed. St. Louis, MO: Institute of Jesuit Sources, 1980; *Recollections and Reflections of Pedro Arrupe, SJ.* Yolanda T. DeMola, trans. Wilmington, DE: Michael Glazier, 1986.

11. At the forefront of the development of an ecological consciousness in Catholic circles is Thomas Berry. Any of his works may be recommended. See his *The Dream of the Earth*. San Francisco: Sierra Club Books, 1988. Some of the works of Matthew Fox may be helpful, as well. See also Sallie McFague, *The Body of God: An Ecological Theology*. Minneapolis: Fortress, 1993.

12. LaCugna, p. 304.

13. For example, see Leonardo Boff, *Church: Charism and Power*. New York: Crossroad, 1985.

14. The theme of the true self in Thomas Merton is given systematic treatment in Anne E. Carr, *A Search for Wisdom and Spirit: Thomas Merton's Theology of the Self*. Notre Dame, IN: University of Notre Dame Press, 1989.

15. See H. John McDargh's treatment of psychology and spirituality in *The New Dictionary of Catholic Spirituality*. Michael Downey, ed. Collegeville, MN: Liturgical Press, 1993, pp. 792–800. Follow references in McDargh's bibliography. See also Janet Ruffing, "Psychology as a Resource for Christian Spirituality." *Horizons* 17/1 (1990), pp. 47–59.

16. Some helpful distinctions have been drawn by Carolyn Gratton. For example, see her *The Art of Spiritual Guidance: A Contemporary Approach to Growing in the Spirit*. New York: Crossroad, 1992.

17. See any of the works of Joann Wolski Conn, notably J. W. Conn, ed., *Women's Spirituality: Resources for Christian Development*. Introduction. Mahwah, NJ: Paulist, 1986; 2nd ed., 1996.

18. See James Empereur, "Personality Types" in *The New Dictionary of Catholic Spirituality*, pp. 736–740. Follow Empereur's bibliography.

19. For a brief critique of this tendency, see Kenneth Leech, "Is Spiritual Direction Losing Its Bearings?" *The Tablet* 247/7971 (22 May 1993), p. 634.

■ *Chapter 5: For Further Reading* ■

Carol J. Adams, ed., *Ecofeminism and the Sacred*. New York: Continuum, 1993.

Michel Bavarel, *New Communities, New Ministries: The Church Resurgent in Asia, Africa, and Latin America*. Francis Martin, trans. Maryknoll, NY: Orbis, 1983.

Leonardo Boff, *Ecclesiogenesis: The Base Communities Reinvent the Church*. Maryknoll, NY: Orbis, 1986.

Leonardo Boff, *Ecology and Liberation: A New Paradigm*. Maryknoll, NY: Orbis, 1995.

Lavinia Byrne, ed., *The Hidden Tradition: Women's Spiritual Writings Rediscovered: An Anthology*. New York: Crossroad, 1991.

Joann Wolski Conn, *Spirituality and Personal Maturity*. Lanham, MD: University Press of America, 1994.

Joann Wolski Conn, *Women's Spirituality: Resources for Christian Development*. Mahwah, NJ: Paulist, 1986; 2nd ed., 1996.

Charles Cummings, *Eco-spirituality: Toward a Reverent Life*. Mahwah, NJ: Paulist, 1991.

Michael Downey, *Worship: At the Margins: Spirituality and Liturgy*. Washington, DC: Pastoral Press, 1994.

Richard N. Fragomeni and John T. Pawlikowski, eds., *The Ecological Challenge: Ethical, Liturgical, and Spiritual Responses*. Collegeville, MN: Liturgical Press, 1994.

Roberto S. Goizueta, *Caminemos con Jesús: Toward a Hispanic/Latino Theology of Accompaniment*. Maryknoll, NY: Orbis, 1995.

Kay Leigh Hagan, ed., *Women Respond to the Men's Movement: A Feminist Collection*. San Francisco: Harper, 1992.

John C. Haughey, ed., *The Faith That Does Justice: Examining the Christian Sources for Social Change*. New York: Paulist Press, 1977.

Margaret Hebblethwaite, *Base Communities: An Introduction*. Mahwah, NJ: Paulist, 1994.

Elizabeth A. Johnson, *Women, Earth, and Creator Spirit*. Mahwah, NJ: Paulist, 1993.

Shannon Jung, *We Are Home: A Spirituality of the Environment*. Mahwah, NJ: Paulist, 1993.

Fred Kammer, *Doing Faithjustice: An Introduction to Catholic Social Thought*. Mahwah, NJ: Paulist, 1991.

Belden Lane, *Landscapes of the Sacred: Geography and Narrative in American Spirituality*. Mahwah, NJ: Paulist, 1988.

Richard Rohr, *Discovering the Enneagram: An Ancient Tool, a New Spiritual Journey*. New York: Crossroad, 1992.

Richard Rohr, *Enneagram II: Advancing Spiritual Discernment*. New York: Crossroad, 1995.

Richard Rohr and Joseph Martos, *The Wild Man's Journey: Reflections on Male Spirituality*. Cincinnati: Saint Anthony Messenger Press, 1992.

Rosemary Radford Ruether, *Gaia and God: An Ecofeminist Theology of Earth Healing*. San Francisco: Harper, 1992.

Sandra M. Schneiders, *Beyond Patching: Faith and Feminism in the Catholic Church*. Mahwah, NJ: Paulist, 1991.

Sandra M. Schneiders, "Feminist Spirituality" in *The New Dictionary of Catholic Spirituality*. Michael Downey, ed. Collegeville, MN: Liturgical Press, 1993, pp. 394–406.

Jon Sobrino, *Spirituality of Liberation: Toward Political Holiness*. Maryknoll, NY: Orbis, 1988.

Miriam Therese Winter, et al., eds., *Defecting in Place: Women Claiming Responsibility for Their Own Spiritual Lives*. New York: Crossroad, 1994.

Suzanne Zuercher, *Enneagram Spirituality: From Compulsion to Contemplation*. Notre Dame, IN: Ave Maria Press, 1992.

Suzanne Zuercher, *Enneagram Companions*. Notre Dame, IN: Ave Maria Press, 1993.

CHAPTER 6

Studying Spirituality

One of the most significant developments in Christian spirituality today is the emergence of the study of spirituality in a disciplined way. Today there is a greater recognition that the term "Christian spirituality" refers to both a lived experience and to a rigorous study of this subject. The purpose of this chapter is to describe various methods in studying Christian spirituality, different approaches to understanding Christian religious experience as such. The intention here is not to engage in purely academic and theoretical issues. It is rather to draw attention to the fact that understanding Christian spirituality is a vital part of any serious approach to living the Christian spiritual life. If the spiritual life is to be understood, then some measure of disciplined study is necessary. Further, spirituality studies can also be helpful in separating wheat from chaff. This is all the more important today in the face of the spirituality sprawl. The insights of scholars engaged in the study of spirituality can be most helpful to others who are trying to understand spirituality and to grow in the spiritual life.

Our focus in this chapter will be on what those who actually study spirituality are saying about the subject of their study. Among the contributors to the development of the study of Christian spirituality Sandra Schneiders has, by far, brought the greatest measure of clarity on this subject. It should be noted at the outset that even though the major focus of this chapter is on the study of Christian spirituality, most of those studying this subject attend to the broad range of spiritual experience within which the experience of Christian spiritual life is best understood.

115

The fact that the study of spirituality is emerging as a distinct discipline should not obscure the fact that spirituality was studied rigorously in earlier periods. Any pre-Vatican II priest would have had on his bookshelf, alongside his *Manuale Theologiae Dogmaticae*, and his *Manuale Theologiae Moralis*, a copy of his *Manuale Theologiae Ascetico-Mysticae*. In addition there were the standard manuals of spirituality, such as those of de Guibert, Garrigou-Lagrange, and Tanquerey. Though intended as practical guides in the spiritual life as well as in the life of virtue judged to be central to it, these works and others like them were the fruit of rigorous scholarly discipline. But shifting currents and perspectives on the experience of the Spirit since the Second Vatican Council have called for new methods of reflection and integration. In the years following the council there emerged new methods and approaches in the study of scripture, morality, liturgy, and systematic theology. Much the same is just now occurring in the study of spirituality.

Spirituality is no longer tethered to the notion that priests and religious are the only ones who are called to the fullness of the spiritual life, or that married people must somehow get over that disability in order to develop and mature in the ways of the Spirit. Now a variety of persons and groups find the Spirit awash in a great diversity of situations. And so in recent years considerably more attention has been given to the issue of the precise limits and scope of spirituality (content) and the steps (methods) which might be taken in studying this subject. In studying spirituality today, a great deal of attention has been given to answering two interrelated questions: 1) *What* is studied in studying spirituality? 2) *How* is it to be studied? Struggling with these questions has resulted in the emergence of very different views of just what the "stuff" of spirituality is, and how one might best approach it. And as the *what* and *how* of studying spirituality becomes clearer, it is increasingly recognized as a distinct branch of study in both pastoral and scholarly circles.

In the scholarly study of spirituality there has been a strong turn to the history of spirituality, to take account of the diversity of experiences and traditions and of things unnoticed. But slowly different methods of reflection are emerging. Sandra Schneiders, Walter Principe, Bernard McGinn, and Joann Wolski

Conn have in different ways sought to bring methodological form to the scholarly discipline of spirituality studies. Efforts such as theirs notwithstanding, spirituality is still a fledgling discipline. Unlike systematic theology, considered by many to be real "bread and butter theology," the content of spirituality is often thought to be fluff, its methods murky. Perhaps this is because there is general agreement that however important the study of spirituality might be, living in Christ through the presence of the Spirit is far more important than the academic study of it. Even scholars in the field of spirituality would agree that it is more important to live the spiritual life than to study it.

Systematic theologians in the postconciliar period have recognized experience as the locus of revelation and the relationship with God. Karl Rahner, Edward Schillebeeckx, Gustavo Gutiérrez and others have generated spiritualities, and methods of reflecting on spiritual experience, out of their theologies. Since moral theology or ethics is that area of theological inquiry concerned with the actual living of the Christian life, many continue to argue that spirituality is a specialization within the larger province of moral theology or ethics. Indeed, from a Christian perspective it is altogether true that living the good life requires individual and communal prayer. At the same time our efforts to live a good life give shape to our prayer.[1] But the question of the precise nature of the relationship between systematic theology or moral theology and spirituality has been a catalyst for recent efforts to identify the precise content of spirituality studies and the strategies by which spirituality can best be understood. Caution must be taken in the face of the tendency to allow spirituality studies to drift back—or worse, to be forced back—under the tutelage of systematic theology or moral theology. But if spirituality is to find its own footing as a distinctive area of inquiry and study after years of functioning as a subdivision of moral theology, at least one crucial question must be answered precisely: Just what is it that the study or the discipline of Christian spirituality studies? This is inextricably linked to the question of how the subject is approached.

In spelling out what distinguishes this field of inquiry from other disciplines, the following features stand forth.

The subject matter of the study of Christian spirituality is Christian religious experience as such. More precisely it is concerned with the Christian spiritual life as experience. In this view, because the experience is *Christian*, theological insights and accuracy are a vital part of the study. Because it is *spiritual*, this study must attend to the human spirit and the Spirit of God, with equal attention given to both. Because it is concerned with life, it is not focused primarily upon rare or extraordinary phenomena, but upon the whole of life as an existential project. And because it is concerned with *experience* as such, it must be attentive to the whole range of human experience, affective as well as cognitional, communal as well as individual. Precisely because the study of Christian spirituality is concerned with the experience of self-transcendence and personal integration in light of the ultimate value with which one is concerned, or the highest value which one perceives, all dimensions of human life are within its purview. It must allow within its scope absolutely everything that pertains to the task of personal integration in light of levels of reality not immediately apparent.[2]

Consequently, no one discipline of study will do justice to the complexity of this subject. Insights are necessarily drawn from anthropology and sociology, aesthetics and studies of language, psychology and history, just to name a few. The study of spirituality must be an interdisciplinary discipline, a "field-encompassing field."[3] But here caution needs to be taken lest the net be cast too wide, and the language of spirituality be used to describe such a broad spectrum of realities that it refers to nothing specific or clearly identifiable.

Clarity is emerging regarding the specific content of spirituality, the *what* of spirituality studies. But there is still room for clarification on the meaning of such terms as "experience" and "spiritual," complex realities that do not yield easily to precise and tightly knit definitions. This is to acknowledge that there is still a measure of ambiguity in the emergent discipline of spirituality studies. Some are inclined to lament the absence of precision. But understood more positively, a certain lack of precision at this stage of its development is to be expected precisely because the focus of spirituality studies is the spiritual life as experience, a thick and dynamic reality not easily harnessed by concepts and language.

It is true that there is no generally accepted definition of spirituality or Christian spirituality at this time. But it is possible to provide a brief description as follows.

The study of Christian spirituality is concerned with the human person in relation to God. While this may be said to be the concern of any area of theology or religious studies, it is the specific concern of the discipline of spirituality to focus precisely upon the relational and personal (inclusive of the social and political) dimensions of the human person's relationship to God.

Earlier distinctions between the *credenda*, what is to be believed (the domain of dogmatic or systematic theology), and the *agenda*, what is to be done as a result of belief (the domain of moral theology), are not always as clear as they may seem. The discipline of spirituality has developed out of moral theology's concern for the *agenda* of Christian living. But the focus in the study of Christian spirituality is on the full spectrum of those realities that constitute the *agendum* of a Christian life in relation to God, including the *credenda*. Thus, the relationship between spirituality and biblical theology, systematic theology, moral theology, pastoral theology, and liturgical studies is stressed. What differentiates spirituality from, say, systematic theology or moral theology, is the dynamic and concrete character of the relationship of the human person to God in actual life situations. Moreover, the relationship is one of development, of growth in the life of faith, and thus covers the whole of life. Spirituality concerns religious experience as such, not just concepts or obligations.

The study of spirituality in the postconciliar period is an interdisciplinary enterprise. Scholars in the field tend to bring insights from other disciplines (e.g., sociology, history, economics, especially psychology) as any one or several of these may contribute to a fuller understanding of the subject at hand. Additionally, the fruits of ecumenical and interreligious dialogues are brought to bear on the subject where appropriate.

In an effort to arrive at greater precision regarding the "stuff" of spirituality, just *what* spirituality studies, I have identified seven focal points of investigation. These seven focal points might be envisioned as *where* one looks in studying Christian spirituality.

Christian spirituality as disciplined study is concerned with the Christian spiritual life as experienced in persons. In other words, Christian spirituality is concerned with the work of the Holy Spirit in tensive interaction with the human spirit: 1) within a culture; 2) in relation to a tradition; 3) in light of contemporary events, hopes, sufferings and promises; 4) in remembrance of Jesus Christ; 5) in efforts to combine elements of action and contemplation; 6) with respect to charism and community; 7) as expressed and authenticated in praxis.

Such a framework can be used by those who are studying spirituality in a disciplined way, as well as by those who are simply attempting to come to a deeper understanding of spirituality, their own or others', past or present. It is important to note here that the study of Christian spirituality is not concerned simply with the examination of written texts. One of the great riches of Christian spirituality is the range of genres in which the Christian spiritual life is expressed. To consider only written texts is to leave too much out of the loop. So whether one examines a scriptural or theological text, a legend of a saint or a painting of her with eyes turned heavenward, a type of religious vesture or sacred music, a kind of church architecture or sculpture, stained glass windows in a cathedral, dance, or the enactment of a rite, it is useful to consider the object of study in view of these seven focal points. One might ask: What was the *culture* within which this depiction of the Last Judgment was painted? When considering a treatise on virtue, one might ask: What are the religious and theological *traditions* reflected, adhered to, departed from in this text? What are/were the significant *events, hopes, sufferings, and promises of the age* in which this score of sacred music was composed? How does it reflect, nuance or critique them? How is the *memory of Christ* expressed, or what is the dominant image of Christ being expressed, in this bronze? What is the view of the relationship between *contemplation and action* expressed in this stained glass depiction of Mary with book-in-hand? Or with Jesus in her arms? Or with hands folded in prayer? What is the understanding of *charism and community* expressed in the uniform attire of women religious prior to the Second Vatican Council? And what understandings of charism and community are expressed in the very different attire of women religious today? These are just a very few of the type of questions that might be raised in trying to uncover the specific spirituality of a person or group, past or present.

How might one work within this framework when considering a text or life of an individual of an earlier epoch? As an example one might focus on the life of Francis of Assisi and the early Franciscan writings. In trying to understand Francis' spirituality, one could consider the way in which Francis remembers Christ, or try to uncover the predominant image of Christ that emerges in early Franciscan writings and devotion, e.g., the poor Christ crucified. By way of contrast one might then focus on what can be known of how Christ was remembered, or what image of Christ predominated, in the legacy of Dominic and his first followers. Whatever similarities there may be, there are significant differences in the way Christ was remembered by Dominic and the early Dominicans on the one hand, and by Francis and his followers on the other. And the praxis (the seventh focal point of the framework) of the gospel appropriate to a Dominican, i.e., preaching, teaching, study, will be somewhat different from the praxis appropriate to a Franciscan. This is due, at least in part, to the way Christ is remembered, or which image of Christ predominates, in each tradition. Said another way, there are distinctively Dominican and Franciscan spiritualities due to the fact that the central understanding of Christ that lies at the heart of each is quite different. One might then juxtapose these insights alongside what may be gleaned from a reading of the Ignatian sources in view of the question of how Christ is portrayed therein, attentive to what have been judged appropriate forms of praxis that result from such a remembrance. The same might be done when looking to the life and writings of some more contemporary figures such as Dorothy Day, Roger Schutz, Jean Vanier or Thomas Merton.

If one were to shift attention to a contemporary text such as the United States Catholic Bishops' pastoral letter on the economy,

Economic Justice For All, with an eye to the spirituality expressed in its pages, it might be useful to consider the understanding of culture (the first focal point) operative therein. How is the Spirit at work within a culture shaped by materialism, consumerism, pragmatism? Where is the work of the Spirit in those economic systems that systematically impoverish one culture at the expense of another? How is the Spirit expressed and authenticated in the praxis of the gospel amidst conflicts of impinging cultures replete with economic ambiguities.

As another example of the attempt to understand a contemporary text, person, or movement, when considering Christian feminist spirituality one might focus on the role of tradition (the second focal point) in women's spirituality. How has the Spirit been at work in those Christian traditions that have rendered the voices and experiences of women inaudible and insignificant? How has the Spirit enabled women to resist, critique, and/or reject those traditions by which they have been willfully and systematically excluded?

Whether the focus be on the past or the present, using this framework enables one to attend to the crucial importance of praxis as the expression and authentication of the Spirit's work (the seventh focal point). The praxis appropriate to a person or group, past or present, will vary due to the way in which the Spirit is at work within a culture, in relation to a tradition, in response to the events, hopes, sufferings, and promises of an age, in view of different ways of remembering Jesus, in efforts to combine elements of action and contemplation, and with respect to diverse charisms and different constellations of community. Thus, the praxis of the Christian life, or spirituality, appropriate to the members of an enclosed monastic community of Cistercians will be quite different from that of the members of the Catholic Worker House due, in no small measure, to different perceptions of how action and contemplation are to be integrated within a life project in response to the work of the Holy Spirit.

This framework, *where* one looks in studying Christian spirituality, may be employed no matter *how* one approaches the subject. It is to the issue of precisely *how* one goes about studying the Christian spiritual life that we now turn.

HOW IS SPIRITUALITY STUDIED?
METHODS AND EMERGENT APPROACHES

How is spirituality to be studied? It is possible to identify at least four methods in studying Christian spirituality today: the theological, the anthropological, the historical, and the appropriative.[1] Each of these four has a clear methodology, a precise series of steps and stages followed in a patterned, predictable, repeatable fashion in order to yield results, i.e., a clearer understanding of the Christian spiritual life. In addition to these, I have identified five other approaches to Christian spirituality which are yet emerging. They are less methodologically mature than the others. Indeed it is arguable whether these five approaches are methodological at all. These emergent approaches may be referred to in terms of a governing concern at the heart of each: feminism, liberation, ecological consciousness, cultural pluralism, and marginality. These approaches appear to be based upon a central concern rather than a methodology. For example, feminist writers employ theological, historical, and anthropological methods but with a particular lens. The same might be said for liberationist writers. But at this stage in the development of the study of Christian spirituality these approaches are worthy of note, because the attention given to the governing concern in each one calls for new methods of investigation and articulation, all the while bringing greater methodological form to them.

In describing the four major methods in the study of spirituality, a cautionary note is in order. In understanding Christian spirituality, no one of these approaches is complete in itself. They are best viewed as interrelated and mutually complementary. For example, the theological approach must be attentive to human experience precisely within the context of a community of faith in history. Likewise, approaches which focus on history must give due attention to the beliefs of a historical community as well as to the theology which reflects on these. And so while it is incumbent upon those who study spirituality to be clear about the strengths and weaknesses of a particular method and to sharpen their methodological repertoire, it is altogether necessary that they continually recognize the advantages of the other methods in spirituality studies.

Each method emphasizes a certain dimension of the experience of the Christian spiritual life. In other words, there is in each one a central governing concern.

1. The Theological Method

The first method, the *theological*, is the one with the deepest roots in the Christian tradition. It is the most prevalent of the four major methods in studying spirituality. The principal concern here is with the practice of the Christian faith, implementing in the practical order that which has been revealed in Christ. The spiritual life is the Christian life in practice through the grace of the Holy Spirit. Here the spiritual life is viewed in terms of the gradual formation of the human person by grace and Spirit, the transformation of human nature into a new creation. Spirituality is understood as the living out of what theology and morality have articulated in concepts, theories, and principles. In such an approach, both systematic theology and moral theology are viewed as having already established the principles for understanding and practicing spirituality. At the heart of this method is some understanding of central Christian doctrines: Trinity, Christ, church, sacraments, grace—indeed the whole spectrum of the Christian mysteries—which are assumed to be normative for evaluating and judging the authenticity of spirituality. This is the real advantage of this method. But because spirituality is concerned with experience as such, and not first and foremost with theories, concepts, principles and obligations, when employing the theological method care must be taken not to allow theological presuppositions to unduly dictate and restrict spiritual experience or the understanding of spirituality. The tendency is to judge all spiritual experience by the criteria of a particular Christian theology. Spiritual experience that does not fit into such a theological construct is either dismissed out of hand or seen as somehow less spiritual or less authentic than the spirituality of those who are explicitly Christian, or those who adhere to a particular set of theological convictions.

When experience is to the fore in understanding spirituality, as it should be in any approach to the study of spirituality, then theology need not dictate or determine what is experienced. Rather it helps clarify, evaluate, support, challenge, and sometimes correct the experience of persons and groups, past or present.

What then is the role of theology vis-à-vis Christian spirituality?[5] Spirituality is not a subdivision of either dogmatic theology or moral theology. Spirituality is being freed from its tutelage to both, and is emerging as a partner with them in the larger arena of all those disciplines which fit under the wide umbrella of theology or theological studies. And as a partner, theology (in the narrow sense of dogmatic or systematic theology) has a crucial contribution to offer to spirituality and to the study of this subject. For if spirituality is concerned with self-transcendence and personal integration in light of levels of reality not immediately apparent, or in view of the highest ideals and ultimate values perceived, then theology in the strict sense of reflecting upon, formulating and communicating those highest ideals and ultimate values, is a vital part of the larger enterprise of studying spirituality. To view the relationship of theology and spirituality in these terms is not to advocate a return to the practice of placing spirituality under the aegis of dogmatic and moral theology. It is, rather, to recognize that there exists a relationship of reciprocity and critical correlation between the two.

There is a dialectic between theology and spiritual experience. Theology can judge experience; experience can stretch theology; a given theology can make certain experiences possible. A Buddhist, for example, isn't likely to experience a personal God. A Christian who is formed in an appropriate theology of the Trinity, on the other hand, is more likely to experience God as a communion of persons in loving relation. Thus, there is a sense in which theology does heavily influence, if not dictate, spiritual experience. But if one recognizes a dialectical relationship between theology and spirituality, then theology not only evaluates, supports, challenges, critiques, and corrects expressions of spirituality, but theology is itself shaped and changed as new experiences in the spiritual life evaluate, support, challenge, critique, and correct it. This becomes clearer when we consider the way in which emergent experiences of the Christian spiritual life are shaping new approaches to the theological task.

2. The Historical Method

The second major method in the study of Christian spirituality is the *historical*. The fundamental convictions and orientations of the historical method underpin the great studies of the history of Christian spirituality which began to appear in the first half of this century, most notably the monumental *Dictionnaire de spiritualité*, a work begun in 1932 and undertaken over several decades.[6] This has been followed by sweeping surveys such as the work of Louis Bouyer and his collaborators. Their multivolume *A History of Christian Spirituality* surveys the whole history of spirituality through the optic of its linear and organic development.[7] But sweeping surveys tend to oversimplify highly complex historical developments. Contemporary historical approaches tend to avoid sweeping surveys, and focus rather on individuals, particular movements, specific topics and issues.[8] But the focus is often limited to historical texts, with the bulk of attention given to the difficult task of interpreting historical texts in context.

The governing concern in the historical approach is to gain access to authentic spiritual experience by way of an examination of documents or texts which recount the spiritual experience of those who have gone before us. The guiding conviction here is that these texts do in fact provide the most, if not the only, reliable access to authentic spiritual experience which the texts themselves verify as such.[9]

The advantage of this approach is that it provides a safeguard against the all-too-common inclination toward "presentism," a tendency to disregard the insights, perceptions, convictions, and shortcomings of earlier epochs as old-fashioned, irrelevant, and unable to speak to our experience. The historical method serves as a reminder that contemporary efforts to live the Christian spiritual life do not occur in isolation. We stand in continuity with many who have gone before us. Their experience can enlighten, instruct, guide, challenge, or validate our own. And so an awareness and appreciation of history is altogether essential in studying and understanding spirituality.

The problem with the historical approach in many of its expressions, however, lies in the assumption that a historical text or document gives access to the actual spiritual experience of persons and groups from some earlier epoch. But it does not. What the text provides is an account of spiritual experience. The historical approach, then, may be too narrow if its focus is solely on texts or documents of earlier epochs. Spirituality as a disciplined study must cast the net wider because of the recognition that Christian spiritual experience is not reducible to the history of Christian spirituality as this is expressed in historical texts. To the question of whether there is anything aside from historical texts and documents to be studied in the emergent discipline of Christian spirituality, the only appropriate answer is a resounding yes!

3. The Anthropological Method

The third method in the study of spirituality is the *anthropological*. Here the point of entry is neither theological reflection nor analysis of historical texts, but the human person's experience in its own right. The central concern is to attend to human experience precisely as spiritual experience. Human experience as spiritual experience is the very "stuff" of the study of spirituality. The very structures and dynamics of the human person precisely as human make possible the quest for self-transcendence in knowledge, freedom, and love. In other words, human experience in and of itself is transcendentally directed. As such, authentic human experience is *ipso facto* spiritual experience.

In the anthropological method, spirituality characterizes us first as human rather than as religious or Christian. In this view, being explicitly religious or Christian is simply an actualization of the human capacity for self-transcendence, i.e., one expression of spirituality. This broadly-based anthropological approach views Christian spirituality as a specification of religious spirituality, which is itself one specification of the actualization of the human spirit or human spirituality. "Christian spirituality is 'only' human spirituality in its most universal, inclusive, and progressive expression."[10] From this perspective, spirituality is an element of human life as such. The true nature of the human being as such, i.e., precisely as human, is that which is realized or actualized through knowledge, freedom, and love in the task of self-transcendence and personal integration. This actualization may occur in explicit relation to God. In that instance the spirituality would be specifically religious. And when it is realized in relation to God in Jesus Christ through the Spirit at work in the community of disciples, the church, then the spirituality is explicitly Christian.

From this broadly-based anthropological approach, the subject of spirituality is not limited to either religious or Christian expressions. The study of spirituality, even and especially Christian spirituality, requires an appreciation of all expressions of the human spirit. Thus, spirituality is not a discipline concerned simply with the practice of the faith through the implementation of already revealed and received theological truths and moral principles.

Studying spirituality in this way, then, requires attention to the whole range of human experience. And this demands that the study of spirituality be cross-cultural, interdisciplinary, and inter-religious, since what is at issue here is not just this or that kind of religious or spiritual experience, but experience in and of itself. The broadest possible range of insight and perspective is to be brought to the fore in this approach to spirituality studies.

The strength of this approach is that it attempts to give attention to the full range of human experience. In principle, nothing is ruled out of bounds. Everything in the human enterprise is to be brought under consideration. There is no prior judgment about what authentic spiritual experience is, or about what kind of experience is spiritual "stuff." In this approach, the task is to be more descriptive than prescriptive, more constructive than analytical.

But there may be a weakness in this overriding concern to be attentive to the broad spectrum of experience. There is a tendency here to let spiritual experience free-float, perhaps avoiding the task of rigorous discernment and judgment in the face of the various expressions of the human spirit's striving. How, for example, might we be sure that the values we perceive and pursue in the quest for personal integration through self-transcendence are indeed truly valuable? There remains in this approach a need for a clear articulation of the normative criteria by which authentic spiritual experience, precisely as human experience, might be recognized as such.

4. The Appropriative Method

The fourth major method in studying spirituality is the *appropriative*, which has a certain affinity with the anthropological method. But here the governing concern is understanding the Christian spiritual life as experience. This understanding occurs through interpretation and application. The purpose of interpretation and application is appropriation, i.e., real understanding that is not just notional or theoretical but transformational. Texts, art, music, persons, architecture, dance, popular devotions, liturgical rites, and so on are painstakingly interpreted so that their meanings might be understood. The core conviction which drives this method is that all genuine understanding is transformative. In other words, when meanings, purposes, and values are appropriated, i.e., understood "from the inside out," they transform. But this requires much more than a literal reading of a text. It demands interpreting a spiritual experience or movement, past or present, in such a way that we allow our own preconceptions and tightly held convictions to be called into question by them. Interpretation is no easy matter since there are questions behind every text. One thus not only interprets the written text but must also examine the silences, what is not said, what is assumed. What are the questions which prompted the text to begin with? The issue of silence becomes important in reappropriating voices which have been lost or ignored in the Christian tradition.

The appropriative method involves three interrelated steps. First, one seeks to describe the spiritual life as experienced. Since the concern is with the broad range of experience, spiritual experience must be attended to in all its complexity. Here the insights of various branches of study such as psychology, medicine, sociology, economics, can be most helpful, as well as the perspectives of those of different cultures and religious traditions. All these can be instructive in the effort to describe the experience of the spiritual life, or one or another instance, manifestation, or expression of it.

The second step in this strategy is critical analysis. Not only is theological criticism to be brought to bear at this stage. One might also bring the insights of contemporary psychological investigations to bear on manifestations of spiritual experience in the past or in the present. For example, some expressions of asceticism such as prolonged fasting which are detailed in the writings of some mystics are to be regarded with some suspicion in light of contemporary insights regarding the psychosocial dynamics of anorexia. Likewise, some expressions of religious obedience in the spiritual practices of earlier epochs are suspect when viewed in light of contemporary investigations into the nature of personal maturity and communal responsibility. A critical reading demands that one wrestle vigorously with the object of interpretation so that it might yield authentic meanings.

The third step in such an approach is that of constructive interpretation. In looking to Christian spiritual life as experience, the aim is not simply to describe it or to critique it. These are necessary steps. But the aim in this method is the transformation and expansion of the person in and through understanding by way of appropriating meaning. Through the rigorous work of description and critique, the interpreter constructs an understanding of the Christian spiritual life. Hard won insights based on description and critique of expressions of the spiritual life past and present provide the interpreter with insights that might help throw light on spirituality today. So the point is not simply to analyze texts from the past, but to correlate insights from the past with present modes of perceiving and living the Christian spiritual life. Understanding and personal transformation occur in this tensive interaction.

If there is a weakness in this method it lies in the assumption that authentic understanding through appropriation of meaning is transformative not just of individual persons but of communities and other larger social bodies. While there may be some truth in this assumption, in my view it is necessary to explicate just how it is that personal transformation might effectively and systematically bring about social transformation.

Recall that each of the four major methods employed in studying Christian spirituality emphasizes a different facet of the experience of Christian spiritual life. There is a governing concern in each. These methods are not mutually exclusive, however. Insights from all four can assist in a deeper understanding of Christian spirituality. In some ways it is true that the most suitable method would be the one which gets the job done. In other words, for some studies the historical method might be the most suitable. If spirituality is an interdisciplinary field, then many disciplines and methods are validly employed.

That having been said, in my judgment the appropriative method is perhaps best suited to the study of Christian spirituality. Because in using this method in the study of Christian spirituality there is an explicit recognition of the reason *why* one is studying Christian spirituality. And the reason is this: To understand the experience of Christian spiritual life, and in understanding this experience in the manner of appropriation, one is thereby transformed.

EMERGING APPROACHES

Recall that the seven focal points as a framework for investigating *where* the Holy Spirit may be at work should be kept in view when relying on any one of the methods already discussed, or on one of the emerging approaches which concern us here.

The emergence of feminist, liberationist, and ecological consciousness, as well as the awareness of cultural pluralism and of many persons and groups marginalized by church and society, require new methods of description, analysis, and interpretation. The approaches to understanding these spiritualities are still emerging. While this can be said of any approach to studying spirituality because the discipline is in many ways still in its adolescence, the five approaches to spirituality to which we now turn are as yet in the early stages of development.

Feminist spirituality should not be confused with the spirituality of women, or women's spirituality.[11] Feminism is a critical worldview which emerges from the experience of being oppressed because one is a woman. Being a woman and oppressed does not make a woman a feminist. And not only women are feminists. What makes one a feminist is the explicit awareness of oppression of women, together with naming patriarchy as the reason for oppression. This calls for adherence to a new way of understanding human beings, and a commitment to implementing a new vision of reality based on this understanding.

Feminism did not begin with religious women. But some of
the women who first began to formulate feminist theory and
spell out an understanding of feminist praxis did have an interest
in religion. As a result, some of the implications of feminist
theory and praxis were grasped quickly by women in the
churches as well as women of other religious persuasions.

The impact of feminism spread rapidly through the Christian
churches. Some women began to articulate their awareness of
oppression because of their sex. They began to retrieve the stories of many women who were often hidden or cast to the margins of the Christian tradition. As women's experience was
slowly and painfully spelled out, it became more and more apparent that many women's experience of God, Christ, church, sacraments, indeed every dimension of the Christian spiritual life,
had been colored by experiences of hiddenness, voicelessness,
marginalization precisely because they were women.

Just as feminist consciousness has called for new methods of
reflection and inquiry in biblical studies, theology, and ethics, feminism requires fresh approaches to the study of the Christian spiritual life as experience. In my view, the governing concern in such
an approach is to recover the neglected and hidden spiritual experience beneath the yoke of women's oppression, and what this says
not just about the spiritual experience of women, but about the
God experienced by them. Indeed, as recent studies have shown,
the central theological question "Who is God?" is answered in
fresh and persuasive ways from a decidedly feminist stance.[12]

Though there is no clearly articulated feminist method for
studying spirituality as such, the contours of a feminist spirituality are, in fact, quite clear. Christian feminist spirituality is
grounded in the experience of oppression and in the struggle for
liberation from it in light of a new vision of human life, history,
world, and church. There is in feminist spirituality a sharp critique of dualist hierarchy, especially the hierarchy of men over
women. This is the root of oppression, the key and paradigmatic
dominative relationship from which other instances of subjec-
tion are derived. Women's bodies have often been thought to be
lesser than men's, and impure because of menstruation, bearing
and giving birth to children.

Thus there is in feminist spiritual experience an explicit commitment to overcome all manner of dualism, particularly the dualism that denigrates materiality and glorifies, by way of sharp contrast, the spirit or the soul. The same dualist mentality which belittles women's bodies has resulted in violating and "using" "lesser" forms of the created order. So just as there is a conscious effort to reintegrate in a holistic way both matter and spirit, body and mind, so is there a strong commitment to nondualist and nondominative relationships with nonhuman life and the whole of creation.

Narrative and ritual play a key role in feminist spirituality. Narrative takes the form of personal stories by or about women told in circles of remembrance. Rituals emphasize participation. Such rituals often stand in marked contrast to the more hierarchical, performative rituals of mainline churches in which the focus is often on a single individual, i.e., the priest or minister.

Finally, from its origins, feminist spirituality has sought to make explicit the relationship between personal growth and the praxis of justice in the social order. This is based on the conviction that the oppression suffered by women is not something which they as persons have brought on themselves. Rather, it is enshrined in the very socio-political, economic, and religious institutions of which they are a part. Hence the feminist insight: The personal is political. Feminist spiritual transformation is at one and the same time personal and social, individual and communal.

Christian feminists, particularly Catholic feminists, have a heavy burden because of the ways in which theology and church structures of ministry, leadership, authority, and decision-making still block the fullness of human flourishing among women. Some have found Christianity, preeminently the Catholic Church, so hopelessly sexist and oppressive that they have moved outside or beyond it for their spiritual survival. Other committed feminists are working for the transformation of the churches from the inside out, so that the liberating gospel can be handed down to the next generation, to our daughters as well as our sons. This sort of Christian feminism has become for an ever-increasing number of women and men a very clear and compelling sign of God's abiding presence in the church and in the world.

A second experience of the Christian spiritual life calling for new approaches and methods of study is the struggle for liberation in the Third World, particularly Latin America. Like feminist spirituality, a *spirituality of liberation* is born in the experience of oppression.[13] In this case, it is the oppression of the poor—women, men, and children. The Word of God in scripture, when heard in the context of poverty and oppression, can offer a liberating and empowering message. The governing concern in this approach to spirituality is to attend to the human struggle for freedom and liberation from all that blocks the fullness of human flourishing as the very work of the Holy Spirit who empowers believers to live and do the truth in love freely.

In liberation spirituality there is a strong sense of the intrinsic connection between liturgy and life, worship and the ethics of daily living. But this intrinsic connection pertains not only to one's individual life, and to the lives of those in one's immediate circle. The encouraging and empowering Word heard and celebrated in worship has an impact on every dimension of life, inclusive of the socio-political and the economic. Consequently, liberation spirituality sees the very "stuff" of transformation to be structural and institutional, as well as personal.

Liberation spirituality is rooted in a sense of God's universal love and offer of salvation. But because the poor and oppressed are often cast to the margins of church and society, liberation spirituality is motivated by the preferential option for the poor. It is in and through God's preferential option for the poor, and through human beings participating in this option, that God's offer of good news and salvation is, in fact, offered to all. It is in and through the poor that God's message of liberation and salvation is offered universally, to the whole world.

The poor and oppressed in their struggle for liberation hold pride of place in this understanding of the experience of the Christian spiritual life. This is for two reasons. First, the sacred scriptures are replete with examples of God's liberating and empowering Word being offered first and foremost to the poor and marginalized, the last and the least. Second, turning to the experience of the poor requires that all mainstream views of God, Christ, church, sacraments, and so forth, be scrutinized. That is to say, the experience of the poor and oppressed prevents those in the mainstream from making an idol of the mainline view of God. Without the alternative experience of God which is given to those who are poor in their struggle for liberation, mainline views of

God may go unchallenged. In such views, God is an absolute monarch whose power is unrestricted. Here God guarantees the preservation of the status quo, and becomes an idol which legitimates the oppression and poverty brought on by the status quo. The experience of the poor and the oppressed demands that the idolatrous God of the mainline be unseated so that all those who believe can attend to the presence of the living God.

In liberation spirituality, solidarity with the poor and the struggle for freedom teaches us not only about the poor, but especially about God. The poor remind us of the otherness and transcendence of God because they challenge us to see that the living God is altogether other than any of the idolatrous views of God which legitimate the status quo, keeping the poor poor and the oppressed at the edges of church and society. Since God gives a liberating and salvific Word first and foremost to the poor and captive, they remind us that God's grace and presence are to be found where least likely expected, calling those at the centers of power in church and society to a radical conversion, to solidarity with the poor and those in bondage, and to a commitment to social transformation as that which constitutes the very heart and soul of the Christian spiritual life.

Liberation spirituality then demands solidarity with the poor and their struggle from oppression as well as commitment to the pursuit of justice that is inclusive of material as well as spiritual needs, attentive to the needs of communities and societies and not just the demands of the individual's rights and liberties.

A third expression of spirituality which calls for new approaches and methods of study is one marked by a strong *ecological consciousness*.[14] Closely related to this is an awareness of the importance of environment, i.e., place, in the shaping of spirituality.[15] Here the governing concern is to attend to the network of relations between human and nonhuman life, recognizing that the Spirit of God is bringing about the salvation of the whole world, not just of human beings. Ecological spirituality is grounded in a firm sense of the gracious character of all life, not just human life. Creation is not just a fact, or a burden, but a gift. Consequently, all creation is to be accepted, affirmed, nurtured, and brought to fulfillment.

Those who experience the sanctity of all life in this wider sense recognize that the way humans treat nonhuman life, the whole natural order, is having terrifying consequences. Human intrusion into the ecological balance has been so harmful to animal, plant, and inanimate life that the damage may be irreversible. The effects of industrial development, pollution, and erosion now threaten the very survival of the natural environment, the matrix of all living things.

An ecological spirituality is not motivated principally by the desire to preserve the natural environment for utilitarian purposes. That is to say, the concern here is not first and foremost to care for the earth because it is useful to human beings since they depend on nonhuman life for their own existence. It is rather that an ecological consciousness is shaped by a strong sense of the sacredness of God's creation, God's presence to all creation. Creation is, consequently, not to be abused. The only appropriate human disposition in relationship to nonhuman life is respect, indeed reverence, instead of domination. It is this sense of reverence, wonder, and awe that makes ecological spirituality a deeply contemplative spirituality. From this point of view, contemplation may be described as a way of being and seeing motivated above all by a nonpragmatic disposition toward others, and toward all created things. In the contemplative life, other persons and things, as well as God, are not looked upon in terms of their usefulness. They are gazed upon, beheld, enjoyed for their own sake. How important it is to be attentive to this newly emerging spirituality in a culture such as ours which is driven by conspicuous capitalist consumerism, a frame of mind in which each and every thing is viewed and calculated in terms of its utility and service of our wants, what it can give us or do for us.

The fourth expression of spirituality that calls for new methods of description, analysis, and interpretation is that colored by an awareness of *cultural pluralism*. In most approaches to religion today there is a recognition of enormous diversity and multiplicity of religious expression. Together with this there is attention to very diverse cultures which give rise to quite different spiritualities. Culture is second nature to human beings. It is the extension and transformation of the "givenness" of the natural order in accord with specifically human purposes. Apple trees are part of the natural order. An apple pie is part of culture. Not only does the apple pie complement a festive meal, it also conveys a wide range of symbolic meanings as exemplified in saying that so-and-so is "as American as motherhood and apple pie." Culture is that whole constellation of means by which a people expresses its fundamental meanings and purposes regarding the most important elements of human living: family, community, progeny, sexuality, social arrangements, their convictions about right and wrong, their sense of the sacred. It is inclusive of art, music, literature, dance, law, ritual, manners, codes of dress, and much more.

In the study of Christian spirituality there is a growing awareness of the importance not just of cultural diversity, but of cultural pluralism.[16] In an approach shaped by an awareness of cultural pluralism, differences are not simply tolerated. Rather, they are deeply appreciated and respected. Diverse and seemingly incompatible cultures are not viewed as irreconcilable, but rather as dialectically inseparable. Each one is looked to as a unique locus for what may be disclosed therein. And each is necessary if our view of the spiritual life as experience is not to be narrow and provincial. The governing concern here is to recognize and appreciate the manifold ways in which spiritualites are mediated by cultures. This is accompanied by a strong measure of vigilance in the face of the tendency to legitimate cultural hegemony in any way. A dominative culture mutes the self-disclosure of the living God present in the universal human struggle for authentic meaning, purpose, and value.

The fifth experience of the Christian spiritual life that calls for new methods of investigation is that of *marginality*.[17] Here the governing concern is to attend to the alternative experience of those who are at the margins, the periphery, of religious institutions and societies. "Margins" describes the edges. The term refers to the blank spaces at the borders of a page, the place where nothing is written, the empty corners. The margins are defined by the center. The center is the place of importance or significance. The margins, by contrast, are insignificant. When applied to persons and groups, those at the margins are the insignificant, the unimportant, the voiceless, the forgotten. Those at the margins of church and society are those whose existence is judged to be less important than that of those at the center, those in the mainstream.

The marginalized have usually been pushed and shoved out of the center because of race, sex, sexual orientation, religious belief, physical or mental handicap, economic status. The reasons for marginalization are beyond counting. By way of contrast to those at the centers of power and influence, those at the margins are often weak and vulnerable—unless and until they begin to accept marginality as a permanent feature of their existence. This entails a recognition that the center can no longer "name" them as marginal, peripheral, voiceless. Such a realization involves the long and painful task of naming and accepting the strengths of the weak and the vulnerable precisely as strengths, precisely by the weak and vulnerable themselves. Thus the edges become the center in light of a new understanding of power which is born in the experience of vulnerability and weakness. Power here is that which enhances the fullness of human flourishing rather than that which dominates and controls others, pushing and shoving those whose lives are different out of the purview of the prestigious and the "powerful."

An approach to Christian spiritual experience motivated by this concern for marginality *begins* by looking to the experience of those who are the last and the least in church and society. That which is described, analyzed, interpreted is the vast array of alternative experiences of the Christian spiritual life as these are brought to voice by the weak and the wounded, those at the periphery, in their own voice and in their own way. Thus, in this approach the focus is on those persons, those events, those movements which have been and continue to be judged as insignificant, unimportant, unworthy. Forgotten. Out of the picture. Here the central conviction is that it is even and especially in the lives of those at the margins, as well as in those marginalized dimensions of ourselves, that something crucial is known about God which cannot be known in any other way.

The emergence of these five approaches to understanding the Christian spiritual life calls for new methods of description, analysis, and interpretation. Recall that what distinguishes these five approaches from the four methods is that the former are not methodological in the strict sense of the term while the latter clearly are.

It may be useful to sound a note of caution here. Each of these five approaches is driven by an overriding concern. This may tend to obfuscate other concerns, different dimensions of the wide range of human experience to be taken up in the quest for integration through self-transcendence. As these emergent approaches gain greater methodological form it will become more and more necessary to make explicit recommendations about how to generate some shared approaches to the Christian spiritual life among diverse groups with divergent concerns— addressing the needs of women *and* people of color *and* children *and* gays *and* lesbians *and* the handicapped *and* the disenfranchised of the Third World *and* nonhuman life forms. At this stage of their development there is in these approaches a heavy dose of the language of victimage. With this comes a measure of one-upmanship, an ever-escalating pitch, as if each one were trying to make a case for the intensity and totality of their suffering. What is required, not simply desirable, as these approaches gain methodological form, is a clearer articulation not only of the desire for freedom from bondage, oppression, and neglect, but also of the nature of the relationship among them all in a shared search for the common good.

TEACHING SPIRITUALITY

Among those engaged in the study of Christian spirituality there is an ongoing question about how Christian spirituality is to be taught, indeed if it can be taught at all.[18] If we follow Saint John Climacus there is a sense in which spirituality, like prayer, cannot be taught. He insists that it is impossible to teach another to pray. He points out that just as no one can teach the blind to see, no one can teach another to pray. But what we can do is encourage those who do have the gift of sight to open their eyes, to look, and to understand.

There is not a strict equation between prayer and spirituality. And so the insight of John Climacus may help only up to a point. Many would agree that there is a need for teachers in the spiritual life. The great religious traditions have master teachers who have guided others along the spiritual path. Indeed the passing on of spiritual traditions may be the oldest discipline in human history. But just how spirituality is to be taught depends on the context or location, and the nature of the relationship between student and teacher. Even more, it depends on the kind of educational environment in which spirituality is being taught.

If the educational context is that of a religiously affiliated college or university, a pastoral center or diocesan institute, a seminary or a monastery, the teaching of spirituality oftentimes has an explicitly formative and confessional character. In such settings, it is usually clear that the teacher of spirituality is exercising a formative influence on the student.

But if the context is that of a major university without formal affiliation with an ecclesial or religious body, i.e., a secular academic setting, then personal religious commitments and spiritual practices are to play no explicit role in the study and teaching of spirituality. Even though the topic of study may be a spiritual text or treatise on the spiritual life, there is an effort to adhere to the canons of objectivity in order to safeguard the integrity of research and investigation. It is widely held that in such an educational environment, the transmission of spirituality as transformative experience is to take place outside the academic setting.

In the first context, the formative dimension of teaching and studying spirituality may run the risk of becoming another form of proselytism. Or it may serve no other purpose than the student's personal self-enrichment. On the other hand, because of the reluctance to allow explicit religious and spiritual commitments in the study of spirituality, the second context may be giving short shrift to the participatory and transformative dimensions which are part and parcel of any quest for understanding, even rigorous "objective" research.

Because spirituality is concerned with the spiritual life as experience, those who are drawn to study and teach this subject usually bring their own experience in the spiritual life to bear in both tasks. People study and teach spirituality because they want to understand, and so be transformed by, spiritual experience. In other words, more than with other disciplines, the study and teaching of spirituality is participatory and self-implicating. But a cautionary word is in order here. The aim of studying spirituality is not the same as that of preaching or catechesis. And the study and teaching of spirituality is not primarily for the purpose of personal development or self-enrichment of the student. Its purpose is to come to a deeper understanding of the spiritual life as experience. To this end, the study and teaching of spirituality necessarily involves three dimensions.[19] Attention to these three elements brings even greater clarity to the question: *Why* study spirituality? Further, *why* teach spirituality?

First, those who study and teach spirituality seek to contribute to the cumulative body of knowledge of the spiritual life. This requires rigorous disciplines of investigation and interpretation so that the experience of the spiritual life can be understood not just by oneself but by others. Second, in gaining a deeper understanding, however, the student and teacher of spirituality finds that he or she is transformed in the process. Third, one's transformative understanding extends well beyond the self through the study and teaching of spirituality through which one contributes to the spiritual growth and development of others.

CONCLUSION

Though Christian spirituality has been the subject of rigorous study in earlier periods of history, the insights and orientations of the Second Vatican Council have called for new methods and approaches in the study of spirituality. We have identified *what* it is that the discipline of spirituality studies, *where* one looks to investigate this subject, *how* the subject is studied, and *why* spirituality is studied and taught.

In closing it may be useful to recall that even the most rigorous and disciplined scholars in the field of Christian spirituality would readily concur that the living of the Christian life has existential and ontological priority over the study of it. But an authentic understanding of the spiritual life as experience, be it our own or that of others past and present, can only be of benefit in our faltering efforts to be conformed to the person of Christ through life in the Spirit.

■ *Notes to Chapter 6* ■

1. For a fine treatment of the reciprocal relationship between moral theology and spirituality see Mark O'Keefe, *Becoming Good, Becoming Holy: On the Relationship of Christian Ethics and Spirituality*. Mahwah, NJ: Paulist, 1995. See also Dennis J. Billy and Donna L. Orsuto, eds., *Spirituality and Morality: Integrating Prayer and Action*. Mahwah, NJ: Paulist, 1996.

2. Sandra M. Schneiders identifies the formal and material object of the study of Christian spirituality in "A Hermeneutical Approach to the Study of Christian Spirituality." *Christian Spirituality Bulletin* 2/1 (Spring 1994), pp. 9–14.

3. Van A. Harvey, *The Historian and the Believer: The Morality of Historical Knowledge and Christian Belief*. Philadelphia: Westminster, 1966, pp. 38–67, especially pp. 54–59.

4. In treating these four methods for the study of Christian spirituality I draw from Sandra M. Schneiders, "A Hermeneutical Approach to the Study of Christian Spirituality." *Christian Spirituality Bulletin* 2/1 (Spring 1994), pp.9–14. Schneiders calls the fourth of these methods the hermeneutical, recognizing some of the problems with the term "hermeneutical." I have opted to call it appropriative, since the objective in this method is not so much interpretation and application as it is transformation through the dynamics of the appropriation of meaning.

5. My own view of the relationship between theology and spirituality has been shaped by the work of Rowan Williams, especially *The Wound of Knowledge: Christian Spirituality from the New Testament to St. John of the Cross*. London: Darton, Longman & Todd, 1979; Boston: Cowley, 1991.

6. M. Viller, F. Cavallera, and J. de Guibert, eds. *Dictionnaire de spiritualité ascétique et mystique. Doctrine et histoire*. Paris: Beauchesne, 1932–1995.

7. Louis Bouyer, et al., *A History of Christian Spirituality*. 3 vols. New York: Seabury, 1963–1969.

8. For a fine example of the use of the historical method in the study of Christian spirituality, see the first two volumes of Bernard McGinn's projected four-volume study, *The Presence of God: A History of Western Christian Mysticism*. Vol. I: *The Foundations of Mysticism: Origins to the Fifth Century*. New York: Crossroad, 1992; Vol. II: *The Growth of*

Mysticism: From Gregory the Great through the Twelfth Century. New York: Crossroad, 1994.

9. David Lonsdale and Philip Endean have criticized the overall conceptualization and execution of *The New Dictionary of Catholic Spirituality*. See Lonsdale, *The Tablet* (25 December 1993/1 January 1994), pp. 1706–1707, and Endean, *The Way* 34/3 (July 1994), p. 250, and *Heythrop Journal* October 1994, pp. 471–472. A less strident critique, but one which is essentially the same, is that of Jackie Hawkins, *Priest and People* 8/12 (December 1994), pp. 489–490. In my view their criticisms are rooted in a particular understanding of spirituality which holds that there is a strict equation between Christian spirituality and the history of Christian spirituality. The view is not uncommon.

10. Richard Woods, *Christian Spirituality: God's Presence through the Ages.* Chicago: Thomas More, 1989, p. 340; rev. ed. Allen, TX: Christian Classics/Thomas More, 1996.

11. For a fine treatment of Christian feminist spirituality see Anne E. Carr, *Transforming Grace: Christian Tradition and Women's Experience.* San Francisco: Harper & Row, 1988; See also Sandra M. Schneiders, *Women and the Word: The Gender of God in the New Testament and the Spirituality of Women.* Mahwah, NJ: Paulist, 1986. I draw from the work of Sandra Schneiders, "Feminist Spirituality" in *The New Dictionary of Catholic Spirituality.* Michael Downey, ed. Collegeville, MN: Liturgical Press, 1993, pp. 394–406.

12. See, for example, Elizabeth A. Johnson, *She Who Is: The Mystery of God in Feminist Theological Discourse.* New York: Crossroad, 1992.

13. For a good example of a Latin American spirituality of liberation see Gustavo Gutiérrez, *We Drink from Our Own Wells: The Spiritual Journey of a People.* Maryknoll, NY: Orbis, 1984; See also Jon Sobrino's essay "Spirituality and the Following of Jesus" in Ignacio Ellacuría and Jon Sobrino, eds., *Mysterium Liberationis: Fundamental Concepts in Liberation Theology.* Maryknoll, NY: Orbis, 1993, pp. 677–701; see also Roberto S. Goizueta, *Caminemos con Jesús: Toward a Hispanic/Latino Theology of Accompaniment.* Maryknoll, NY: Orbis, 1995.

14. A fine example of an ecological spirituality is Leonardo Boff, *Ecology and Liberation: A New Paradigm.* John Cumming, trans. Maryknoll, NY: Orbis, 1995, especially Part Three, "From World Consciousness to Mysticism."

15. For example, see Belden Lane, *Landscapes of the Sacred: Geography and Narrative in American Spirituality*. Mahwah, NJ: Paulist, 1988.

16. For a clarification of this difference see Diana L. Eck, *Encountering God: A Spiritual Journey from Bozeman to Banaras*. Boston: Beacon, 1993.

17. Rebecca Chopp has developed a hermeneutics of marginality in *The Power to Speak: Feminism, Language, God*. New York: Crossroad, 1989. See especially pp. 43–46. See also Michael Downey, *Worship: At the Margins: Spirituality and Liturgy*. Washington, DC: Pastoral Press, 1994. In developing my own approach to the issue of marginality I am indebted to the work of Elizabeth Janeway, *Powers of the Weak*. New York: Knopf, 1980.

18. For differing perspectives on teaching spirituality, see Bernard McGinn, "The Letter and the Spirit: Spirituality as an Academic Discipline." *Christian Spirituality Bulletin* 1/2 (Fall 1993), pp. 1, 3–10; Sandra M. Schneiders, "Spirituality as an Academic Discipline: Reflections from Experience." *Christian Spirituality Bulletin* 1/2 (Fall 1993), pp. 10–15; James A. Wiseman, "Teaching Spiritual Theology: Methodological Reflections." *Spirituality Today* 41 (1989), pp. 143–159.

19. Schneiders refers to the aim of studying spirituality in terms of the "irreducibly triple finality" of the discipline of Christian spirituality. Sandra M. Schneiders, "Spirituality in the Academy." *Theological Studies* 50/4 (1989), p. 695.

■ *Chapter 6: For Further Reading* ■

Christian Spirituality Bulletin: The Journal of the Society for the Study of Christian Spirituality provides consistently good essays that address the specific issues pertinent to the study of Christian spirituality.

Modern Christian Spirituality: Methodological and Historical Essays. Bradley C. Hanson, ed. American Academy of Religion Studies in Religion, no. 62. Atlanta, GA: Scholars Press, 1990.

CHAPTER 7

An Informed Spirituality

What is the understanding of Christian spirituality that emerges from these pages? If we are to avoid the excessive rigidity and the saccharine piety that characterized many approaches to Christian spirituality in the past, spirituality must be at once deeply affective and sober. And if it is to be discriminating in the face of the various movements and currents in the spirituality sprawl today, it must be informed. What are the features of a mature and authentic Christian spirituality informed by the understanding of spirituality discussed in these pages?

An informed Christian spirituality is rooted in a holistic understanding of the human person. It begins with experience. Great attention is given to the contextual and relational dimensions of spirituality, inclusive of intimacy and sexuality. The relational matrix of all Christian spirituality is the life of the Trinity itself, a communion of persons both divine and human in loving relation. This is to say, that all Christian spirituality is *ipso facto* trinitarian. Because Christian spirituality is easily untethered from its trinitarian moorings, an informed spirituality must recognize the formative task of theology and its crucial role in the development of the spiritual life.

There is stress on the liturgical and scriptural foundations of spirituality. And there is a recognition of the universal call to holiness, thereby undercutting the notion of a spiritual elite. Spiritualities for clergy and religious share this sensibility. As in every age, there is attention to the search for the true self, but with greater appreciation for the complementarity of human and

145

spiritual development. In the quest for the true self, self-scrutiny and the development of critical consciousness vis-à-vis the sources of oppression and injustice go hand in hand. There is the effort to find modes of integrating prayer and prophetic service as expressions of the faith that does justice appropriate to the urgent demands of the age. Among these urgent demands is the promotion of the full equality of women in church and society. Greater attention is given to those who have been marginalized and, consequently, whose alternative experience has been rendered voiceless and insignificant by the dominant social-symbolic order in church and society.

At the brink of the third millennium, more, but still insufficient, attention is being given to the appropriate Christian response in the face of scientific and technological developments, as well as to the possibility of nuclear terrorism and the probability of ecological crises of proportions heretofore unimaginable. There is a fuller recognition of both the riches and the shortcomings of Christian history and tradition for answering the problems to be faced in the third millennium. Finally, there is a deeper recognition that the work of the Spirit is not confined to the church, but is operative in a variety of religious traditions and in diverse cultures, thus calling for a greater measure of cooperation among Christians and others in the promotion of authentic human flourishing.

On the basis of the understanding of Christian spirituality spelled out in these pages, it is now possible to formulate guiding principles for contemporary Christians who seek to live in the presence and by the power of Christ's Spirit.

GUIDING PRINCIPLES FOR A CHRISTIAN SPIRITUALITY

1. Spirituality is not one dimension of the Christian life. It *is* the Christian life in the presence and by the power of the Holy Spirit; being conformed to the person of Christ and united in communion with God and others. Personal integration takes place in and through conformity to the person of Christ.

2. God comes to be known and loved first and foremost in the experience of human relationship. God's initiative toward us is

the basis for any relationship between human beings and God. As a result, prayer, religious discipline, celebration in Word and sacrament, spiritual growth and maturation, all rest on the action and presence of God in our regard.

3. A Christian spirituality must be firmly anchored in the Christian story wherein God is revealed to be the God of Jesus Christ, by the power of the Holy Spirit. The symbols, images, and concepts appropriate to a Christian spirituality emerge from the story of God's action in history and presence to creation, and ordinarily will be drawn from the scriptures and from other Christian writers.

4. Christian spirituality is an invitation to participate in the very life of God through communion with the Incarnate Word by the power of the Holy Spirit who is love. Such participation brings the Christian into the heart of the mystery of God's own life. The call to ever deeper communion with God is at the same time the call to ever deeper communion with others.

5. Christian spirituality develops through the life of prayer, which is the ongoing cultivation of relationship with God rooted in God's being toward us. The spiritual life is sustained and flourishes by the continuing call of the God who is recognized as active in history and present to creation, and by gradual appropriation of the salvific gift offered in the life and ministry, crucifixion and resurrection of Christ.

6. Christian holiness involves growth in conformity to our true selves as human beings created for union with God. We are oriented in the very depths of our being toward this union. Deification, or being made divine, entails conformity to the true self, our true humanity.

7. Christian spirituality involves attention to the many dimensions of the human person and of the God-world relation, not just the interior dimension, or the inner life of the human person. A contemporary spirituality entails greater attention to a wide range of factors that together constitute the human being's relationship with self, others, and God. It is inclusive of the social,

political, and economic realms; in a word, *every* dimension of personal and communal life is involved in a Christian spirituality.

8. Because the mystery of God grounds the communion of all persons, the spirituality to which it gives rise is singularly attentive to the quality of relationship between and among human persons, as well as to their relationships with various other creatures and goods of the earth. Everything that exists originates from a relational God, and exists in relation to the whole and its various parts, so that relational interdependence is a keynote of this spirituality. Such a spirituality is critical of modes of relationship built on domination/submission, power/powerlessness, or activity/passivity. Since the relational pattern of divine life is the norm of human life, relationships that respect difference, nurture reciprocity, and cultivate authentic complementarity are revelatory of divine life.

9. Those who espouse a Christian spirituality must be attentive to building equitable relationships between and among persons who may appear vastly unequal in terms of economic, social, mental, or physical ability. Christian spirituality is to be explicitly inclusive of those who are broken, wounded, needy, or disabled. By virtue of their participation in the very life of God, each and every person possesses a dignity that goes beyond social standing or function.

10. Christian spirituality is one of solidarity between and among persons. It is a way of living the gospel attentive to the requirements of justice, understood as rightly ordered relationships between and among persons. This entails working to overcome obstacles to full human flourishing posed by evil and sin. Sin may be understood as the failure to discern and build a community of rightly ordered relationships, the inability or unwillingness to respect the interdependence of all human and nonhuman life, and as the divisiveness that ruptures the harmony between God and human beings. A Christian spirituality entails a commitment to live in rightly ordered relationship with self, others, and God. The restoration of such rightly ordered relationships is the

meaning of salvation, and involves not only the individual but has wide-ranging implications for social forms of life.

11. A Christian spirituality is wholly oriented to the God who is its source and end. It is a way of living through participation in the very life of God by communion with the Word of God in the power of the Holy Spirit, and in communion with all creatures. Prayer, ascetical discipline, study, apostolic activity, the rigors of marriage and family life, ministry, the works of mercy, and especially the celebration of the paschal mystery in Word and sacrament, all increase participation in divine life. Deeper participation in the life of God is, of course, recognized in the fruits born in our being with others as God is with us.

12. The traditional sharp contrast between active and contemplative forms of spirituality no longer can be upheld. Contemplation of God should lead to loving action on the behalf of others, and Christian action should be rooted in the insights of contemplative living.

13. The God who dwells in light inaccessible cannot be controlled or dissected by Christian theology, nor fully grasped within a Christian spirituality. The mystery of God elicits a contemplative gaze and the prayer of quiet repose rather than analysis, systematic scrutiny, or theological assertion. Nor can God be controlled by the canons of pragmatism and productivity. Similarly, the mystery of God cannot be controlled or thoroughly analyzed within any one religious tradition. Hence the importance of recognizing the insights of various religious traditions and diverse cultures in order to come to a fuller understanding of the mystery of God. In the ecumenical and interreligious dialogues, consideration needs to be given to the question of whether doctrinal differences among religious traditions can be or ought to be reconciled by finding convergences in spiritual experiences.

14. Christian spirituality lived out in the order of creation gives rise to a lively sense of stewardship for the goods of creation. This is fertile ground for exploring the relationship between human and nonhuman life in such a way as to throw

light on current ecological themes such as the interdependence of various forms of life.

15. Contemplative prayer understood as nonpragmatic regard for created reality reaches its fullest expression in mystical experience which alone stands to eradicate narcissism, pragmatism, and unrelenting restlessness, which block full participation in the divine life. Authentic social and cultural transformation require spiritual transformation in and through contemplation of the unfathomable mystery immutably disclosed in Christ through the Spirit of God, Spirit of Christ.

CONCLUSION

The purpose of this chapter has been to suggest that a contemporary Christian spirituality needs to be an informed spirituality. In drawing attention to the guiding principles for Christian spirituality today, the intention has not been to provide parameters for determining what is authentic spirituality and what is not. It is rather more a matter of trying to point out several *jalons de route* or signposts along the way for those who are trying to understand Christian spirituality today. This understanding will itself undergo revision as we continue to grow in deeper understanding and fuller appropriation of the presence and action of the Spirit. No doubt our understanding of the spiritual life will grow and develop, especially as we stretch to make enough room for the silence in which true understanding is born. And through which it endures.

Index